ELVIS PRESLEY

.

ELVIS PRESLEY

A Biography

Kathleen Tracy

GREENWOOD BIOGRAPHIES

GREENWOOD PRESS
WESTPORT, CONNECTICUT • LONDON

Library of Congress Cataloging-in-Publication Data

Tracy, Kathleen.
    Elvis Presley : a biography / Kathleen Tracy.
        p. cm. — (Greenwood biographies, ISSN 1540–4900)
    Includes bibliographical references and index.
    ISBN 0–313–33827–2 (alk. paper)
    1. Presley, Elvis, 1935-1977. 2. Rock musicians—United States—Biography. I. Title.
    ML420 . P96T73 2007
    782.42166092—dc22
    [B]   2006025381

British Library Cataloguing in Publication Data is available.

Library of Congress Catalog Card Number: 2006025381

ISBN–13: 978–0–313–33827–4
ISBN–10: 0–313–33827–2
ISSN: 1540–4900

First published in 2007

Greenwood Press, 88 Post Road West, Westport, CT 06881
An imprint of Greenwood Publishing Group, Inc.

www.greenwood.com

Printed in the United States of America

The paper used in this book complies with the Permanent Paper Standard issued by the
National Information Standards Organization (Z39.48–1984).

10 9 8 7 6 5 4 3 2 1

CONTENTS

CONTENTS

Photo essay follows page 68.

SERIES FOREWORD

In response to high school and public library needs, Greenwood developed this distinguished series of full-length biographies specifically for student use. Prepared by field experts and professionals, these engaging biographies are tailored for high school students who need challenging yet accessible biographies. Ideal for secondary school assignments, the length, format and subject areas are designed to meet educators' requirements and students' interests.

Greenwood offers an extensive selection of biographies spanning all curriculum related subject areas including social studies, the sciences, literature and the arts, history and politics, as well as popular culture, covering public figures and famous personalities from all time periods and backgrounds, both historic and contemporary, who have made an impact on American and/or world culture. Greenwood biographies were chosen based on comprehensive feedback from librarians and educators. Consideration was given to both curriculum relevance and inherent interest. The result is an intriguing mix of the well known and the unexpected, the saints and sinners from long-ago history and contemporary pop culture. Readers will find a wide array of subject choices from fascinating crime figures like Al Capone to inspiring pioneers like Margaret Mead, from the greatest minds of our time like Stephen Hawking to the most amazing success stories of our day like J.K. Rowling.

While the emphasis is on fact, not glorification, the books are meant to be fun to read. Each volume provides in-depth information about the subject's life from birth through childhood, the teen years, and adulthood. A thorough account relates family background and education, traces personal and professional influences, and explores struggles, accomplishments, and contributions. A timeline highlights the most significant life events against a historical perspective. Bibliographies supplement the reference value of each volume.

INTRODUCTION

To some, he's simply the King. To others, he's the poster child of overindulgent excess. But whether viewed as musical pioneer or tragic figure, Elvis remains one of the most influential performers—and cultural catalysts—of the twentieth century. He is the unwitting bridge between the safe, sexless, Pat Boone–style crooner of the conservative Eisenhower era 1950s and the edgy, counterculture performers like Jim Morrison of the late 1960s who not only exuded sexuality but reveled in it.

Despite laying the foundation for generations of entertainers to follow, Elvis himself didn't adapt well to the changing times. His career peaked and waned over little more than a decade, a surprisingly short window considering the Rolling Stones have stayed culturally relevant since 1962, Aerosmith continues to make cutting-edge music more than 30 years after releasing their first album, and Carlos Santana seems immortal.

But almost from the beginning, Elvis seemed destined to remain identified with—and informed by—a particular era, the result of both circumstance and personality. For as groundbreaking as he was, Elvis was not inherently innovative. While his talent as a performer is undisputed, his ambition only went so far. The joy he found in music couldn't compete with the rebellious lure of drugs. Despite being internationally famous, he was still insecure enough to need the constant affirmation of an entourage and to allow his career and life to be dictated by a Svengali manager whose own power depended on keeping Elvis from exerting his. In the end, he was a larger-than-life star without the social, instinctual, or business skills necessary to take command when his life began to spin out of control.

Whether Elvis would have ever become a pop music or cinematic force again—or been relegated to the nostalgia circuit, kept alive in the public eye primarily as tabloid fodder alongside Elizabeth Taylor and Princess Di—will never be known. It's no small irony that by dying young, Elvis became more financially successful than he ever was in life. He also became canonized as a mythic figure—the boy from the wrong side of the tracks who grew up to become King, only to have his reign abruptly cut short. But buried beneath the public image and the hype, the half-truths and the misconceptions, was a tragically all-too-human man-child who had fulfilled his boyhood dreams only to be consumed by them. The intent of this book is to reveal the man beneath the myth and the sometimes heavy price paid for achieving one's goals, so that Elvis's contributions can be appreciated in better perspective and his failings more compassionately understood.

Even though Elvis has permanently left the building, his legacy remains, because for one blinding moment he blazed a trail that left an indelible mark on this country's psyche. But while the icon lives on, what tends to be glossed over is the unlikely story of just how Elvis went from being a sharecropper's son to one of the original American Idols.

Quite simply, we are who we are because of who we were. So to truly appreciate the magnitude of his achievements, and the maddening waste of his self-hastened demise, it's necessary to look in depth at his humble beginnings and the forces that molded Elvis. Only then can his life and career be put into proper perspective.

Unless otherwise noted in the text, all quotes in this book are based on more than 50 hours of interviews conducted with Earl Greenwood, Elvis Presley's cousin and childhood friend who later acted as his unofficial publicist. The quotes are Greenwood's personal recollections of conversations he participated in, overheard, or was directly told about by Elvis and other family members. Additionally, the thoughts attributed to Elvis are based on conversations he had with Greenwood during which Elvis expressed his opinions and feelings on his career, fame, family, and women. The bulk of the interviews were conducted over a three month period from January to March 1989.

TIMELINE: EVENTS IN THE LIFE OF ELVIS PRESLEY

1935   January 8—born in Tupelo, Mississippi.
1947   Gladys buys Elvis his first guitar.
1953   Elvis makes a record of "My Happiness" at Memphis Recording Service for Gladys's birthday.
1954   July 5—Elvis records "That's All Right, Mama."
1955   March 5—first appearance at the Louisiana Hayride.
            Colonel Tom Parker becomes Elvis's manager in August.
            Elvis signs a record deal with RCA.
1956   The Jordanaires become Elvis's back-up band in January.
            Signs movie contract with Hal Wallis and Paramount Studios.
            March 13—first album is released and sells a million copies.
            September 9—appears on the *Ed Sullivan Show*.
            November 16—*Love Me Tender*, his first film, premieres.
1957   Buys Graceland in March.
            Is drafted in December.
1958   Is inducted into the army.
            Elvis's second film, *King Creole*, opens in July.
            Gladys dies August 14.
            Leaves for Germany in September.
1959   January 8—is interviewed by Dick Clark via telephone on *American Bandstand*.
            Meets Priscilla Beaulieu in November.
1960   January 20—Elvis is promoted to sergeant.
            March 5—Elvis is discharged from the army.

        Earns black belt in karate.
1961   Performs concert in Hawaii to raise money for the USS *Arizona*
        monument.
1964   *Viva Las Vegas is released.*
1968   February 1—Lisa Marie is born.
1970   Meets Nixon.
1975   Wins final Grammy for album *How Great Thou Art.*
1977   Elvis dies August 16.
1982   Graceland is opened to the public.

Chapter 1

THE PRESLEY FAMILY TREE

April 5, 1936, was an unusually muggy spring day, even for Mississippi. The temperature hovered near 90 degrees, and the air was thick and heavy. In her one-room shack, Gladys Presley tried to keep her year-old toddler distracted from the howling wind that shook the building, while keeping herself distracted from the ominous blacks clouds rolling in overhead from the west.

It stormed on and off all day, ragged lances of lightning creasing the dark gray skies, followed by booming thunderclaps that made the ground bounce. The dreary day turned into a wet, unwelcome night, the rain unrelenting.

In the days before Doppler radar enabled meteorologists to more accurately track storm cells and warn those who may be in their path, all that people could do was watch the skies. At night, all they could do was listen. That evening, as many of the local farmers were preparing to go to bed, an eerie silence blanketed Tupelo.

The wind had died down to a mere whisper of a breeze. Not even the crickets were calling. It was as if the night was holding its breath, waiting. Suddenly a roaring fury dropped out of the sky. The sound was deafening, as if a giant freight train was bearing down on Tupelo. Then it exploded, as powerful—and deadly—as a bomb. It was the sound of approaching death.

Terrified people ran out of their homes—some dressed in nightclothes, some with even less. Running as if their lives depended on it (because it did), people raced toward the safety of storm cellars. Those who dared to look saw a black funnel cloud, slithering like a snake, chasing after them across the fields.

Most made it to safety, but hundreds of others didn't. The tornado ripped a swath of destruction through Tupelo, sideswiping the wealthier neighborhoods but savaging the conclaves of poor sharecroppers, white and black, to the west of downtown. One entire family of 13 was killed trying to ride the storm out in their poorly constructed shack.

In all, more than 200 homes were destroyed, 216 people were killed, and 700 others were injured. Had the tornado not skipped over the downtown business district, the tally would have been even higher. Nobody really knows how many others died that night, because in those days blacks were not included in official tallies. As it was, the Tupelo tornado remains the fourth deadliest in American history.

The same storm cell continued east, producing a number of other tornadoes. One of those tornadoes hit Gainesville, Georgia, the following morning, killing 203 people when it plundered the business district just as the workday was beginning—making it the fifth deadliest on record.

The super-cell storms produced a total of 10 tornadoes across Mississippi, Tennessee, Alabama, Georgia, and South Carolina. Tupelo, ravaged by a rare F5 tornado with winds spinning at over 261 miles per hour (a force that can literally rip the bark off trees), was the hardest hit.

Scores of injured people poured into local hospitals, which were little more than clinics and not equipped to deal with such an emergency. The overflow of injured were put up in the business buildings downtown, including the courthouse and the movie theater, with emergency crews sterilizing their instruments in the popcorn machine.

Years later, Elvis's father, Vernon, would tell people how he had stayed rooted in front of his house to watch the tornado, while Gladys ran with their baby to the safety of the storm cellar. Gladys had another version, telling Elvis what his daddy didn't mention was that he was so drunk he couldn't quite think fast enough to get out of the way on his own. "I had you in one arm and your daddy in the other. I was so mad at him I was tempted to just leave him and let him get blowed away." After she dragged her husband to the cellar, Gladys added, he "passed out and slept through the whole thing."

The Presleys were among the lucky—their home was spared and all immediate family members were safe and accounted for. But the story about the killer tornado, which all Tupelo youngsters heard—with ever-increasing embellishments—from the time they could understand language, made an indelible mark on Elvis, who grew up constantly reminded that everything a person owned could be snatched without a moment's notice. And since tornadoes are hardly a rare occurrence in Mississippi, he faced his fears with seasonal regularity.

Every time he was hustled down into the storm cellar, huddling with relatives while waiting for the danger to pass, his imagination would run wild. It didn't help that the cellars were like caves, as they were built into the ground and very spooky, especially at night. Nor did it help that the older cousins would tease Elvis, hoping to scare him even more than he already was. They would tell him that if he sneezed, he could cause the cellar to collapse and bury everyone alive. As usual, Gladys would come to his defense and angrily reprimand whoever was teasing her son.

While the great tornado of 1936 would remain an indelible memory for the Presleys, storms were really the least of anybody's worries, because most of their lives were spent just trying to keep their heads above water. Just as today, in the 1930s Mississippi was America's poorest state, having never recovered from the Civil War. Prior to 1860, Mississippi was the fifth-wealthiest state. But 30,000 men from the state died in the Civil War. Those plantation owners who survived were left bankrupt, partly by the emancipation of the slave workforce and partly because Union troops had left much of the state destroyed.

Not much had changed over the next 70 years. Except for the few big landowners, the majority of people in that part of Mississippi were sharecroppers at one time or another, a life filled with hard work and few rewards. In theory, sharecropping was a good idea. In practice, it was another matter.

The system worked this way: A landowner would give out a plot of farmland to anyone willing to work it. The sharecropper would build a one- or two-room shanty near the parcel of farmland, with the understanding that the landowner would share the harvest's profits at the end of the season.

Unfortunately, even at the best of times there were barely enough profits to go around. For most people, sharecropping was just a way to keep food on the table and a roof over their heads, with little hope of ever saving enough money to buy their own land. Vernon Presley always seemed particularly snake-bit. This feeling was due to circumstances: Elvis was the only child and too young to work in the fields, so Vernon had to work the land on his own; Gladys preferred to find work in the one or two local factories or take whatever seamstress jobs she could find.

Even so, the Presleys were frequently on the verge of going under, and quite often they turned to relatives for financial help. Gladys always accepted food or money gratefully, her voice steady but her eyes betraying the humiliation she felt. She knew better than to promise that the loan would be repaid, so instead she offered to do sewing or other tasks as a form of payback. Gladys never shied away from hard work, although she wasn't afraid to let her family know just how hard she toiled.

Gladys would walk back home with her head held high, but her stooped shoulders and shuffling walk gave away the heaviness of her heart, weighted down by poverty made worse by her husband's easygoing acceptance of it. Although amiable and personable, Vernon was also terribly irresponsible, to Gladys's unending embarrassment and dismay. He lacked ambition and was often laid up with what he claimed to be a chronic bad back, but nobody ever knew from what.

Some suspected it was the mere thought of having to pick cotton—the main crop grown around Tupelo at the time—that gave Vernon a pain. It was literally backbreaking work. As a young boy, Elvis would sit perched in his favorite climbing tree, watching local sharecroppers hunched over as they picked the fuzzy cotton bulbs off the low-lying bushes, their hands bloodied and gnarled.

It's not surprising that Elvis decided very early in life that he was not going to be a farmer—from what he could see, people nearly killed themselves working and ended up with nothing to show for it. But he didn't dream of being famous; his goals were much simpler. He wanted to own a gas station and make enough so he and his mom would be able to get by on their own.

For anyone growing up in the grim days of the Depression, simply having three meals a day was a goal seldom achieved. For someone like Elvis, whose family owned little more than the clothes on their backs, owning his own gas station was a fantasy that, at the time, seemed like an impossible dream. So, had anyone suggested that Elvis would become a famous singer, he would have thought him or her seriously mentally impaired. His family had been farmers and ne'er-do-wells for as far back as anyone could remember, and there was no reason to think the future generations would be any different.

FAMILY TREE

While many of the Presleys were indeed transients, Elvis would have been surprised to find out that his family tree was full of interesting characters. Today it's a given that a person's every movement is tracked by someone, but record keeping, especially in the South, was haphazard at best, well into the twentieth century. Still, it is possible to trace Elvis's ancestry back about 200 years. His paternal great-great-great-great-grandfather, a Scotsman named Andrew Presley Jr., was born in 1754. His father, Andrew Sr., had immigrated to North Carolina in 1745 and made his living as a blacksmith.

Just two weeks after the signing of the Declaration of Independence, Andrew Jr., at age 22, bought 150 acres of land in Lancaster County,

South Carolina, where he intended to settle down with his new wife, a young Irish woman whose name has been lost to history. But the War of Independence interrupted his plans, and Andrew dutifully joined the fight. He still managed to visit home often enough to father at least one war baby.

Andrew had great faith in his new country and was a willing soldier, if not a skilled one. He was a private in the Continental army, and family records indicate that he fought with George Washington during his long tour of duty in the Revolutionary War. According to documents attached to his pension records, Andrew also claimed to know General Lighthorse Harry Lee. The highlight of Andrew's service in the army occurred in 1781 at the battle of Etauw Springs, South Carolina, not far from where he and his wife had settled.

Few history books include this skirmish, but it figured quite highly with Andrew. His brigade fought troops led by General Cornwallis, and the battle is said to have lasted 1 hour and 45 minutes. The Continental army's forces succeeded in driving back the British redcoats, who by this time in the conflict were probably fighting without much conviction. Casualties were light on both sides, and the Americans took more than 500 prisoners.

There's an amusing historical footnote that comes to light in an officer's report that turned up, unexplained, in Andrew's personal papers. Because Andrew was illiterate, he could not have written, or even read, the report, so why he kept it is a mystery. Perhaps it was a memento of his greatest day in battle and the adventure that followed.

During the confrontation, Andrew's regiment overran a building the British were using as a base, forcing the redcoats to flee out the back and into the woods. While searching for possible prisoners, the soldiers came across what must have been the officers' quarters, which were well stocked with quality liquor. As the battle raged outside, Andrew and his cohorts settled back in the safety of the building and drank themselves senseless. It was the beginning of a long-standing Presley tradition.

Andrew stayed in the service until the war ended in 1783. He was 29 years old and needed to support his family now that the army wasn't caring for him anymore. Following in his father's footsteps, he looked up the local blacksmith and offered to work for free to learn the trade. After his apprenticeship ended, Andrew set up his own shop and spent the rest of his life in quiet obscurity. He lived comfortably in retirement off the $20-a-month pension he received from the government and died shortly before his 101st birthday.

One of Andrew's children was Dunnan Presley, the war baby born in 1780. Dunnan suffered from a severe case of wanderlust and spent half his life roaming the countryside, although he never traveled more than 120 miles from his birthplace. When he was 20, Dunnan said goodbye to his parents and moved to North Carolina. It can be inferred that the relationship between Andrew, a man who believed in duty and hard work, and his unsettled son might have been strained. Whether Dunnan forfeited his share of Andrew's land by leaving or left because Andrew had no intention of staking him to his own plot is anybody's guess.

In North Carolina, Dunnan earned a living any way he could, taking one odd job after another. He continued to move whenever the urge struck, seldom staying in any one place long enough to establish himself. He never had a penny to spare but did manage to support a family. By the time he was 40 Dunnan had a wife and was the father of two girls and two boys, including Dunnan Jr.

Then tragedy struck. Dunnan's wife died unexpectedly—although typically, the records fail to say why. He remarried in 1830 to a woman more than 20 years his junior. Some quick arithmetic indicates his second wife was not much older than his children. Dunnan and his young bride had three sons over the next 10 years.

In 1836, Dunnan, along with his wife and their children, and his children by his first wife, who hadn't yet moved out on their own, relocated to Georgia, drawn by the belief—completely mistaken—that the government was giving away free land. Despite his bitter disappointment when he found no free handout, Dunnan tried to make a go of it. But he quickly grew disenchanted and uprooted his family again and headed to Polk County, Tennessee.

An 1850 census report paints a sad picture. Now nearly 70, Dunnan was as poor as always. He owned no land, and his net personal property was worth all of $250. He died later that same year and was buried in a pauper's grave.

Dunnan Presley Jr. was born in Madison, Tennessee, in 1827. Like his father and grandfather before him, Dunnan Jr. was illiterate. On the few occasions it was necessary, he signed his name with an X. Dunnan Jr. was a low point in Presley family history. There's not much good to be said about him. He was a bigamist and twice an army deserter.

Junior's first army desertion dates back to the Mexican-American War, when he was just 20. Joining the army probably seemed like a good idea at the time, but Dunnan Jr. decided fairly soon after enlisting that he wasn't overly fond of being shot at. He was a private in Company C of the Fifth Tennessee Infantry when he went AWOL and took off for home. But he was quickly caught and spent a short time in military jail before being sent back to the front. The government was surprisingly forgiving, because when Dunnan Jr. was mustered out in 1848, he received two dollars for clothing and a land grant of 160 acres.

In 1861, Dunnan Jr. married Elvis's great-great-grandmother, Martha Jane Wesson, in Itawamba County, Mississippi. Interestingly, the evidence clearly shows that he was already married with at least one child—Dunnan III—with that family living in Tennessee. It also appears that each wife knew of the other.

On May 11, 1863, Junior joined Company E of the regiment of the Mississippi Cavalry as a corporal. Not only was the government generous, it had a short memory—Junior had left his last tenure as a private. He enlisted for a year and received $300 for supplying his own horse. True to form, Dunnan Jr. deserted the next month. But this time when he took off, he deserted his family as well, leaving Martha and their two small daughters to fend for themselves in Fulton, Mississippi.

All told, Dunnan Jr. was married four times. Whether he was ever divorced is another matter. His last wife, Harriet, was 20 when they were wed in 1882; Dunnan Jr. was 55. They settled in Brown County, Missouri, and Dunnan Jr. died eighteen years later in 1900.

One of Junior's children from his marriage to Martha was Rosella Presley, born in 1862. Whether out of rebellion against her father's bigamist ways, stubbornness, or indifference to social mores, Rosella bore 10 children out of wedlock over a 28-year period. What was equally shocking for the neighbors was that she gave the children her last name instead of the fathers' names.

An unwed mother of 10, Rosella was not able to provide much for her children. They were poor as dirt with no hope of getting anything better. Being bastards, the kids suffered the sharp barbs of disapproval of the local townspeople. Even so, Rosella was considered a caring mother who did the best she could in raising her children. She taught them to be polite and to fear God, and she took them to church every Sunday until they moved away on their own. She died at 63, without ever revealing the identity of her children's father or fathers—even to them.

Rosella's son Jesse was her one problem child who never did learn the fear of God. Jesse Presley, called J. D., was born in Itawamba County, Mississippi, in 1896. As a youth, he was a hellion; as an adult, he was a hard-working, hard-drinking, and hard-living hell raiser who created more than his share of shock and gossip. Whenever J. D. didn't come home at night, it was a safe bet he was either out carousing with some woman of questionable reputation or sleeping off a bender at the local jail.

Growing up, J. D. had always been restless. To him, sitting in a classroom all day was a waste of time. Against his mother's wishes, he left school at the age of 11 to find a job; he was a willing worker, more interested in a quick buck than a steady future.

When he was just 17, J. D. married Minnie Mae Hood of nearby Fulton, Mississippi. Minnie Mae was 25 and on the plain side, but she also came from a family with money. Whether J. D. married for love has always been a matter of family debate, but he certainly succeeded in marrying well.

Supposedly, Minnie Mae's hand in marriage included a dowry, but it wasn't long before the newlyweds settled into the hand-to-mouth existence that seemed the Presley lot in life. Minnie Mae would have other hardships to bear besides worrying about money. J. D. was a good-looking man with a love for nice clothes—and women other than his wife.

More than one local wondered how J. D. managed to maintain his dapper wardrobe. He drifted from job to job and apparently never had two dimes to spare, but his clothes were always of the nicest quality. Some whispered that he made extra money as a moonshiner, but if this was true he was never caught. J. D. and Minnie Mae raised five children: two sons, Vester and Vernon, and three daughters, Delta Nashville, Gladys, and Dixie.

Even as he aged, J. D. was still considered one of the most handsome men in the area. So when he decided he had grown bored with Minnie—after 30 years of marriage—J. D. filed for divorce, claiming that Minnie Mae had deserted *him*. Outraged, Minnie wrote a scathing letter to J. D.'s attorney charging that it was her husband who had walked out on *her*. Regardless, the judge ruled in favor of J. D. and granted him the divorce. A short time later, J. D. married Vera Pruitt, and they moved to Louisville, Kentucky, where he became a night watchman.

Where the Presley family tree gets murky is when it comes to Vernon's sister Dixie. According to Earl Greenwood, who claimed to be Elvis's cousin, Dixie was one of the family's best-kept secrets, carefully hidden away in the family closet for decades because she spent the last years of her life languishing in a mental institution and died there.

"Mental illness was a shameful thing to many people," Greenwood explained. "If someone in your family was known to be institutionalized, it cast a cloud over the rest of you. Making matters even worse was the fact that Dixie's illness had been caused by an untreated bout of syphilis. In a small town where everybody knows their neighbors' business, it meant a scandal of major proportions."

Greenwood said Dixie simply ceased to exist to her family. Vernon never spoke about Dixie after she left, nor did they include her in any family remembrance. But before she was institutionalized, Dixie married Tom Greenwood, and they had seven children. Since her husband remained healthy, it was assumed Dixie had contracted syphilis via adultery, further adding to the family's shame. When her illness progressed, she was spirited off in the middle of the night to the closest mental ward in nearby Jackson, with the family offering curious neighbors the explanation that she was off visiting relatives. But she was gone—never to be seen again.

Physically, Vernon Elvis Presley was a chip off the old block, having inherited J. D.'s handsome features. But the similarities between father and son stopped there. Vernon was a dreamer who preferred to pass the time watching the clouds roll by while he was fishing, rather than break his back working in the fields. Since he'd grown up poor, he expected nothing different out of life.

Vernon's aversion to work—and what J. D. perceived to be a lack of personal pride—had always been a source of irritation to J. D., and their relationship was strained. Once, when Vernon was just 15, J. D. kicked him out of the house after some disagreement. Vernon stayed with relatives until J. D. cooled down enough for him to return home. But Vernon never expressed anger or hard feelings about his father to anyone. Instead, he just swallowed his bad feelings and kept them buried inside—a trait he would one day pass along to his own son.

Whether it was love at first sight, lust, or an act of rebellion, Vernon shocked everyone in his family by marrying Gladys Love Smith. A vibrant 21-year-old girl who loved dancing and music, Gladys moved with her family to Tupelo in the spring of 1933 from nearby West Point shortly after her father, Robert Smith, died of pneumonia. She was working in a garment factory when she met Vernon at the First Assembly of God church one Sunday.

Vernon was smitten with her prettiness and worldliness. Compared with the other girls he had known, she seemed very sophisticated. Young Gladys had a laugh that sounded like the tinkling of crystal and a strength and belief in the future that drew Vernon to her.

In the first days of their courtship, Gladys couldn't see beyond Vernon's handsome face and endearing gentleness. On a more basic level, their physical passion for one another was apparent to anyone who saw them together. She also found herself caught up in his sweet daydreams and let herself believe that he had the wherewithal to make them come true. They fed off each other's dreams, and the headiness of first love made them believe they could overcome their surroundings and move up in the world.

They eloped a few months later, just shortly after Vernon's 17th birthday. For the rest of her life, Gladys lied about her age, not wanting to be thought of as a cradle robber for marrying an underage teenager.

J. D. was furious at Vernon for running off to marry a girl he barely knew, partly because he didn't believe his son was capable of responsibly supporting a family—a view few disagreed with. But because Gladys was new in town, she and her family weren't familiar with the Presleys and believed she had a fairly good catch in Vernon. He was personable, attractive, and already a skilled carpenter, although he'd make little use of this talent during his life. Like most people in Mississippi, the Presleys were sharecroppers who lived a humble existence, but Gladys believed Vernon shared her desperate desire to improve their social standing. Gladys never bargained for the severe poverty that would dog them until Elvis turned their lives around. Once Vernon was confronted by the effort of turning their youthful dreams to reality, he would quickly be content to let his fantasies live on in his mind only.

It wasn't long after they married that Gladys began to realize her new husband simply was not an ambitious young man or a particularly robust one. He was unable to work for long stretches because of his bad back. Instead, Vernon was the king of the odd job, preferring to flit here and there rather than seek out permanent employment. Part of Gladys's paycheck went to help support her family, so she and Vernon were chronically strapped for money.

Gladys was lovely and vivacious when she married Vernon, but within a short time her looks began to fade, along with her hopes for the future. She tried to hide her bitter disappointment under a mask of stoicism, but it oozed out of every pore. The loving tones she once cooed at Vernon turned into clipped responses, and over the years, whatever affection they had for each other was buried beneath an avalanche of frustration.

Chapter 2

A SHORT-LIVED HONEYMOON

After Vernon and Gladys married, their first priority was finding a place to live. Neither of their parents' homes was big enough to accommodate them, so the newlyweds stayed with friends until Vernon built a two-room shack off Old Saltillo Road on the property of Orville Bean. Bean, a wealthy local landowner, was also Vernon's brother-in-law, which is why he allowed Vernon to remain even though he rarely worked the fields. While Gladys knew they were fortunate to have a roof over their heads, she deeply resented Bean's limited generosity and complained more than once: "Oh, he'll offer you jus' enough so you feel you owe him, but not enough to really help. Rich folks jus' like keepin' you on a string."

She eyed Bean's nice house with envy and wished Vernon had the ambition to ask his brother-in-law for full-time work or at least a plot of their very own. But Vernon wouldn't, and as her hopes for a better life dimmed, Gladys felt the walls of their shack closing in on her. But she refused to give up and tried to convince herself things would get better . . . they *had* to.

She worked hard to make their simple two-room house comfortable. She scrubbed it from top to bottom, stuffed rags in the cracks between the warped boards that Vernon had used as building material, and filled old milk bottles with wildflowers to brighten the otherwise drab and depressing interior. Then in the spring of 1934, Gladys discovered she was pregnant and saw it as an omen—maybe starting a family would get Vernon moving and get their dreams back on track.

Despite their limited resources, Vernon and Gladys were both thrilled with impending parenthood. Pregnancy seemed to recharge Gladys, and after a few weeks of mild morning sickness, she basked in the glow of knowing there was a child growing inside her. She kept her job in the dress factory well into the pregnancy, cheerfully saying the several miles she walked each way to work and back was good exercise for her. She also believed it would keep her strong and healthy for future pregnancies. Next to being financially comfortable, Gladys's biggest wish was to have a large family.

For his part, Vernon couldn't help but think that having a lot of kids would mean more hands down the road to work in the fields. That would translate into more family income and take some of the pressure off him and his aching back. So although for different reasons, Gladys's pregnancy represented the young couple's hope for the future.

Elvis Aron Presley was born around noon on a cold, windswept winter's day, January 8, 1935. It was a long, hard labor and difficult birth for Gladys, who lost a great deal of blood. The doctor had been surprised to discover Gladys was carrying twins. According to family members, Elvis was delivered first and his twin brother arrived minutes later, stillborn.

So instead of being a joyous occasion, Elvis's birth was tempered by the death of his brother. While Vernon struggled in vain to comfort his wife, Gladys clung to her surviving child, blocking everything and everyone else out. The doctor finally had to pry baby Elvis out of her arms to clean him off and wrap a blanket around him.

Vernon and Gladys named their dead son Jesse Garon, and the following day he was laid out in a tiny coffin in their small shanty. The Presleys were so poor that the local church donated both the coffin and a plot of land in the closest cemetery, which was also owned by the church. After a sad funeral attended only by Vernon and Gladys, Jesse was buried the very next day in an unmarked grave. The Smiths, Presleys, and Greenwoods were all surprised at Gladys's vehemence that they not attend, but she preferred grieving in private and expected everyone to respect her wishes. Weak and in pain, Gladys shuffled to the cemetery, insisting on carrying Elvis the whole way there and back, even though Vernon repeatedly offered to help.

Infant mortality rates in Mississippi during the Depression were particularly high, so every expectant mother knew there was a risk of losing a baby. Jesse's death shook Gladys's very soul. She tried to overcome her heartbreak by pouring every ounce of love and devotion in her being onto Elvis, although she often dwelt even more on the baby she'd never hold.

Except for her interaction with Elvis, Gladys remained distant from and uncommunicative with Vernon, who stayed off to the side like some boarder. She rarely even let him hold the baby.

"Vernon would just stand around, shuffling his feet, acting like some stranger who happened by," Nora Greenwood would later remember. "Gladys didn't even notice he was there half the time. He didn't understand she would have come around with some patience. It's no wonder she turned to the baby for comfort—he didn't know how to give her any. But then again, she never gave him the chance, either."

Vernon dealt with his wife's depression by spending most evenings out drinking moonshine with friends. Even though the Twenty-first Amendment had repealed Prohibition in 1933, Mississippi still outlawed the sale of alcohol, so the sharecroppers simply made their own home brew. Of course, this made Gladys more resentful and withdrawn toward her husband and more dependent on her son for love.

It was clear to everyone that the relationship between Gladys and Vernon was never the same after Elvis's birth and Jesse Garon's death. A big chunk of life had gone out of them as individuals and as a couple. Eventually, Gladys confided to friends that the difficult labor and birth had left her unable to have more children, compounding her tragedy. Knowing Elvis was the only child she would raise made her that much more possessive and protective of him. Knowing Jesse Garon never had the chance turned him into an almost mystical figure, a golden child remembered for the man he might have become and the deeds he might have accomplished. Alive in mind alone, Jesse was the perfect child who could never disappoint—an impossible standard for Elvis to try to live up to.

As Elvis grew up, Jesse was an ever-present entity. For as long as he could remember, he had "talked" to Jesse daily, an outgrowth of Gladys's urging Elvis to pray to Jesse and ask him for guidance.

Most children love hearing the story of their birth—all the excitement and funny stories, real or fanciful, that become part of their personal history. Not Elvis. Any mention of his arrival inevitably brought on a wave of melancholy because his entry into the world had been accompanied by death. One part of him never learned to control the guilt he felt over being the one who had lived, while the "better one" had died.

On a more spiritual level, Elvis saw Jesse as his other half. Each was part of a whole that could never be complete until they reunited in the hereafter. Believing that half his soul died at birth would later prevent Elvis from ever fully enjoying the good things that happened to him. "If only Jesse could be here" would become a constant refrain once Elvis's career had taken off.

A big part of Elvis's obsession with Jesse Garon was his belief that they had been identical twins. Even though the doctor who delivered the babies told Vernon and Gladys it was impossible to tell, Elvis was adamant they had been: "Even if nobody else knows, I do. I can feel it. There's no mistaking it."

In later years, it would become a source of intense frustration to Elvis that he was never able to locate his brother's grave site. The issue came up after his mother passed away and Elvis wanted to have Jesse reburied next to her. But by then, Vernon claimed to have no recollection, explaining to a furiously disbelieving Elvis that the grave never had a headstone because they hadn't been able to afford one, and the years had taken a toll on his memory. Local records, especially on pauper's graves, were spotty, and since only he and Gladys had attended the burial service, there was nobody else to ask.

Elvis was a cute, chubby baby who grew into a toddler of fair complexion with blonde hair and enormous, penetrating blue eyes. He had full lips and a wide nose that seemed too big on such a little boy's face.

Growing up, Gladys had dreamed of being a dancer. But if dance was her first love, music was a close second. Gladys claimed she knew from the time he was barely able to walk that Elvis had been born with a gift for music. She'd later say that when she'd take Elvis to church, he'd squirm in her lap whenever the singing started. "He tried singin' before he could even talk … Elvis got a knack for it and the voice of an angel."

One of Gladys's favorite stories was about the time a three-year-old Elvis jumped off her lap and ran up and down the church aisle, singing and dancing to the hymns. Since he was only three and didn't know the words to the songs, he just kind of babbled along, pleasing Gladys to no end (although it's doubtful the rest of the congregation was so enamored).

Even though it might have felt to the local young people that they were growing up in the middle of nowhere, compared with neighboring towns, Tupelo was one of the region's bigger towns. A farming community of about 6,000 people, Tupelo was the county seat and had a relatively bustling downtown, with a movie theater, a Montgomery Ward department store, a general store, and a pharmacy. The rest of Tupelo was made up of farmland that was the livelihood of sharecroppers.

Once away from downtown, most of the roads were unpaved and made of dirt or gravel that kicked up choking dust in the summer and turned into rivers of mud during the spring rains. The church was located away from downtown, as was the dress factory where Gladys had worked. Despite Tupelo's relative size, it was an extremely poor area. But then again, the people of Mississippi were used to being poor. For most of the residents there was nowhere to go, and no way to get where one might have wanted to go.

Not only were Elvis's formative years spent growing up in the hardships of the Great Depression, Mississippi was also enduring a brutal drought.

Conditions became so dire that the federal government stepped in and formed a work labor force called the Works Projects Administration (WPA). The work could be anything from fixing local roads to cutting back dangerously combustible brush, but it paid $20 a week, which was a princely sum to the struggling sharecroppers, who signed up for WPA work in addition to working the fields.

Except for the big landowners, such as Orville Bean, everyone Elvis knew was poor, but even he could see that his family was among the poorest. Because Gladys was reluctant to leave Elvis to go back to work, the burden of supporting the family fell solely on Vernon's shoulders, and he sagged under the weight. To her endless humiliation, Gladys could feel the pity from her friends and neighbors, who felt sorry for her because of her husband's inability to keep a steady job. She couldn't afford to buy a new pair of shoes, and she could hear the whispers when she walked past barefoot down the road in the snow during the dead of winter. Gladys simply pretended not to see the stares or hear the hushed comments and in fact would go out of her way to greet the people she passed. Gladys would never hide her head in shame—that would be admitting defeat.

Although she didn't ask for handouts, she would accept help if offered—grateful but never subservient about it. She refused to believe that this was to forever be her lot in life. But one of the disadvantages of living in a small country town is that everybody knows too much about everybody else, and once a family gets a reputation, it's almost impossible to get out from under it. For as long as they lived there, the Presleys would always be the white trash of Tupelo.

Despite their youth, both Vernon and Gladys aged rapidly after Elvis's birth—Gladys especially. She lost her girlish figure after giving birth and paid less and less attention to her overall appearance. The only thing that mattered was Elvis, who shared his parents' bed, giving Gladys an excuse to put off Vernon's romantic advances. The passion that once engulfed them had dried up and scattered like the dust swirling on the Tupelo landscape.

By the time Elvis was three, Vernon was at the point of desperation—less about money than about the fact that his wife didn't want him physically anymore. Some of his friends pointed out that Gladys might have more passion if Vernon put food on the table regularly.

Vernon's next job was with the Leake and Goodlett lumber company. Driven by either carnal desperation or stupidity, he forged a company check for $100. He was caught within hours, before he even had the chance to spend any of the money. The lumber company owners proved unforgiving and pressed charges. He was found guilty and sentenced to prison, leaving Gladys to deal with the gossip and silent recriminations—and the struggle to survive.

She and Elvis were forced to leave their two-room home and moved in with Ben and Agnes Greenwood. Although she was grateful for their kindness, she withdrew into herself and was drawn that much closer to Elvis, whom she considered literally the only good thing in her life.

Determined to carry her weight, Gladys helped Agnes clean house and cook. In addition, six days a week she would make the rounds to former clients, picking up small sewing and tailoring jobs, which she did late at night, after Elvis was put to bed—her eyes straining to see in the poor light.

In public, Gladys held her head high. She braved her weekly walk to the welfare office with dignity, looking everyone who passed her in the eye. With each trip, however, she seemed to grow visibly older. In private, she wasn't so sturdy, and she turned more and more to Ben's moonshine for comfort. Sometimes the alcohol loosened her tongue and she let herself cry on Agnes's shoulder. "I'd move me and Elvis if we had anyplace to go," she admitted.

Besides alcohol, Gladys found some measure of comfort in church and spent most of her spare time there. Elvis once commented he must have spent more time in church than any child in Mississippi during the time his father was in prison. But he liked the calmness of it and the hymns they sang during services. He was also aware his mother seemed more at peace.

Vernon's conviction resurrected some of the old Presley scandals, such as Rosella's penchant for illegitimate children. Although nobody was in a position to be judgmental—even the poor have their own class distinctions—the Presleys seemed to have sunk to the bottom of the heap.

Although he was only three going on four, Elvis was old enough to feel his mother's tension and knew his father wasn't around because he had done something bad. Gladys hadn't wanted to tell him the truth, but family sentiment prevailed—better he find out from his mama than on the street.

Elvis had always been a personable child, full of laughs and good humor, but during Vernon's absence he became increasingly shy. He walked around like a puppy waiting to be smacked with a newspaper, feeling punished by association.

Most of the time, Gladys absorbed the disapproval from the townsfolk with a steely resolve and adopted an "us versus them" attitude. And she tried to hide her fears and humiliation from Elvis, but occasionally cracks would show, especially after drinking. Anytime Elvis saw his mother cry, he'd burst into terrified tears, too. Gladys would hold him gratefully.

"We don't need nobody but us," she'd tell Elvis at bedtime. And whenever she saw a worried look shadow her young son's face, she'd comfort him by invoking their family protector. "We'll be just fine 'cause we got Jesse looking after us. He's our guardian angel in heaven—and you're mine here on earth."

Gladys clutched Elvis to her side during church services and dared anyone to make a remark to her face. But the effort it took to stand tall in public was exacting a high price. Whether it was caused by the drinking or was just a simultaneous affliction, Gladys's health weakened. She developed a cough that racked her body and stole her breath. Her ankles swelled, and walking became painful. More than once, Agnes and Ben would hear Gladys crying herself to sleep on the couch but were helpless to comfort her.

Elvis became very protective of his mother, to the point that he once took a swipe at Ben when he went to hug Gladys goodnight. Rather than reprimand him, Gladys held him, kissed him, and called him her "little man," a role he would take very seriously from then on.

As he got older, he became even more sharply aware of his family's standing in the eyes of his neighbors, as their remarks became more directed at him personally. They'd call Vernon a jailbird and tell Elvis he was no better. Just as he'd seen Gladys do, he ignored the comments and held his head high—until he was alone. Then there might be tears or, more often in later years, swallowed anger.

Even when groups of boys jumped Elvis or threw rocks at him, he defended himself only just enough to get away. While he might enjoy the fantasy of tying up his tormentors by the local pond at dusk and letting the mosquitoes have at them, he had been raised to turn the other cheek, even if he was provoked. Many times he felt it was a curse to be raised to know better.

While Vernon was serving his time in prison, Gladys found solace in Elvis and, increasingly, in drinking. Even though she drank in private, her bloodshot eyes and the lingering aroma of stale liquor gave her away. She also began missing work, either claiming that Elvis was sick or that she had come down with a migraine.

To everyone's surprise, Vernon's prison term was cut short after he declared his ongoing incarceration was a severe hardship on his family. He arrived back in Tupelo with freshly laundered clothes and two dollars in his pocket, looking none the worse for the wear. Despite having to work in the prison fields—prison officials had no compassion for his bad back—because he'd been fed three meals a day in jail, he actually looked better than when he left.

The same couldn't be said for Gladys. Vernon was shocked at his wife's bloated, haggard appearance. Her once-shiny black hair was streaked with strands of gray, dark hollows beneath her eyes gave her a weather-beaten look, and her skin was splotched with red. Like her sister, Gladys took to eating large chunks of onion, which disguised the smell of the booze but didn't do much for her breath. Even though Ben and Agnes told Vernon about Gladys's drinking, he never discussed it with her. "He'd rather have her soused than on his butt," Ben cynically commented.

Gladys was more relieved than happy to see Vernon. Elvis greeted his father shyly, no doubt sensitive to the tension between his parents. Although he was too young to verbalize it, he'd later admit he harbored his own anger at being left. There were also issues with Vernon being back. Apparently trying to rekindle some of their past passion, Gladys agreed to have Elvis sleep in the other room. For weeks after Vernon's return, Elvis would cry until Gladys brought him back to bed with them.

Whether it was because Vernon had been separated from Elvis during such a pivotal time in his childhood, or because Elvis tended to reflect his mother's feelings more than his dad's, a distance had developed between them that never really went away. Even in an area so poor, fathers would still find the time on occasion to go fishing with their sons or throw a baseball or football around. Elvis and Vernon never shared that kind of companionship, nor did either seem particularly interested in pursuing it.

Elvis did not have close ties to his granddad J. D. Even though J. D. lived nearby, he and Elvis seldom spent any time together. Of course, considering Vernon and J. D. had never been close, it's probably not too surprising. Vernon's jail time had humiliated J. D., and perhaps J. D. assumed that Elvis would be a chip off Vernon's good-for-nothing block and not worth investing any time in. Whatever the reason, the Presley clan seemed happier when they didn't have to deal with one another. Elvis got the feeling that his mother was right—they only really had each other.

For some men, getting out of prison would be a second chance for a fresh start—to learn from their mistakes and use their freedom to make something of themselves. But Vernon was not the introspective type, and about all the experience taught him was not to mess with company checks anymore. He still couldn't hold a job for any consistent length of time, still suffered from his chronic bad back, and still did just enough to get by and little more.

On New Year's Eve in 1940, the people in northeast Mississippi prayed for the next 10 years to be better than the previous 10. As Tupelo rang in

1941, Ben and Agnes hosted a party and invited the other Greenwoods, along with Vernon and his family. Ben's nephew Earl remembers the house was filled with the aroma of baking "that gave us a very safe, secure feeling. The men were playing cards at the dinner table and the women were in the kitchen talking, cooking and quietly toasting out the old year with a few slowly sipped drinks. Since it was a special occasion, Elvis and I were allowed to stay up late. It was a happy night, one of those rare times where you didn't sense that the grown-ups were upset at matters you couldn't begin to understand."

The two young boys wandered into the kitchen to snag some freshly baked bread and sat in the corner eating. Earl says Elvis explained that at midnight they would sing a special song called "Auld Lang Syne" and tried to teach him the words.

"I'll never forget Elvis's clear voice singing me that song, so gently," Greenwood recalled. "His singing voice was high, but incredibly clear. Out of the corner of my eye, I could see Gladys and Agnes turn to listen, and I saw tears in Gladys's eyes.

"Elvis repeated the song to me several times, to the point where I could at least hum the tune close enough to his liking. We each ate another thick slice of bread, followed by a milk chaser. Over the protests of the moms, Ben gave us shot glasses. Elvis played bartender, carefully pouring the milk from a large glass to the two small ones. We prefaced each shot with a robust *Happy New Year!*"

While the two boys toasted each other with milk shots and waited impatiently for midnight, their parents looked forward to the new decade with hope, praying for good health and prosperity—or at least less poverty.

Somebody must have forgotten to pray for peace.

On December 7, 1941, Pearl Harbor was attacked, and a scary quiet silenced Tupelo. Children didn't understand the full implication, but they saw the fear and worry on everyone's face. When the people that children count on to tell them everything is going to be okay are frightened, children know the news isn't good.

The next day, families gathered to listen to the radio and to be close to each other as America formally declared war on Japan. Three days later, President Franklin Roosevelt also declared war on Hitler's Germany and Mussolini's Italy. After years of trying to avoid the conflict raging in Europe, America was now gearing up for war on two fronts.

In Tupelo and across the country, nearly every eligible man enlisted, the anger over the surprise bombing of Pearl Harbor palpable, as was the fear of the country being plunged into war.

While Presley family lore claims Vernon was exempted from the service by declaring his family was totally dependent on him—which would have been the case of most sharecroppers' families—it is more likely that he didn't pass the physical. So he watched as his relatives and friends left to fight in World War II. While nobody wanted the loss of life sure to follow, the war undeniably boosted the local—and national—economy. Although Lee County would remain a poor county, the WPA once again stepped in, creating jobs to help the war effort. Vernon was hired to help build a prisoner-of-war containment facility somewhere in the state, and he stayed with the job until the project's completion, considering it his part of the war effort.

After the first rush of excitement and confusion, the war became a familiar background noise: people were aware it was there, but they paid only marginal attention to it as they went about their daily lives. For Elvis, that meant doing whatever he could to help his mother, in between trying to find time to just have a little fun.

Chapter 3

A GROWING PASSION FOR MUSIC

For as poor as his family might have been, Elvis was always presentable. Regardless of how worn or how old his hand-me-downs were—which mostly consisted of a pair of ill-fitting dungarees and a two-toned shirt—Gladys made sure his clothes were always neat and clean. "You don't need to be rich to look proper," she would always say.

He learned not to complain about always wearing the same clothes day after day, knowing it would just upset his mother and have her calling him an ingrate for not appreciating that she and Vernon were doing the best they could. It made him feel even worse knowing that she often did go without on his behalf.

It was a common sight to see Gladys walking through town wearing several pairs of socks because she didn't have enough money for both of them to get shoes. Elvis would beg her to buy shoes for herself, too, when they were at the secondhand store—partly because he hated her doing without, and partly because he cringed at the stares and whispers that followed his shoeless mother around town. But Gladys was stoic, her explanation a double-edged blade of unconditional love—and manipulation. "It don't matter I go without, just so long as you have . . ." whatever it was she was buying him at that given moment.

The result was that Elvis never got anything he didn't in some way feel guilty about. If he was benefiting, it meant his mother was suffering, somehow, someway. And whether she was aware of it, Gladys never let Elvis forget her sacrifices on his behalf. Even though she loved him with all her heart, part of her couldn't completely overcome that ever-present anger and frustration at being trapped in a life of impoverished hell. If it were just a matter of Vernon, she probably would have left; but with a child, it was too late. Elvis was both her reason to live and her warden, so when he complained, even about the littlest thing, she couldn't help but feel betrayed and unappreciated. In her mind, she had already given up so much for him.

Children intuitively pick up on unspoken attitudes, and Elvis, while he might not have understood its source, translated what he felt into a belief that he was the cause of his mother's troubles and unhappiness. The depth of Elvis's guilt reached its lowest point when he learned the real reason he was an only child.

For years, whenever Elvis would ask why he had no siblings, Gladys would sit him on her lap and give him a big hug. "Because, honey—you's everything we could ever want." But one day when Elvis was eight, Vernon evidently decided his son was old enough to know the truth after Elvis had enthusiastically announced to Gladys for the umpteenth time how much he'd like a baby brother to play with. Vernon took him off to the side and ordered Elvis to stop talking about wanting a brother.

Elvis was confused—other kids had brothers and sisters … why couldn't he?

That's when Vernon told Elvis that after he and Jesse were born, Gladys "had been hurt" inside and now wasn't able to have any more children. The idea that his mother had been hurt in any way upset Elvis. It also made him feel bad that by asking about a baby brother, it made her remember the hurt.

Vernon made Elvis promise to keep their little talk a secret and to stop asking for a baby brother. Elvis kept his promise and never let on to his mother that he knew the truth. In fact, he wouldn't talk about it again until he was a grown man, and then only to select people. But despite his silence, it weighed heavily on his mind over the years and it morphed into an all-encompassing guilt—because of him, his mother couldn't have any more babies. Which is why no matter how much Elvis gave Gladys, how much he doted on her, he could never do enough to make up for all her sacrifices. It also cemented his reliance on the one brother he did have—even though that brother was long dead.

The seeds of future behavior might have been firmly planted in the fertile soil of Elvis's unsuspecting young mind, but their full effect wouldn't show up until later. Despite the pressures of poverty and a tense home life, Elvis was still a kid. He was still capable of putting worries aside long enough to have fun, especially during the summer—if Gladys would let him out of her sight long enough. Because he was an only child, he had to help with all the household chores. But much of the time, Gladys made him stay in simply because she was lonely and she wanted the company, especially when she was cooking dinner. Vernon might have been her husband, but Elvis had become her emotional partner in life.

On days Elvis did have time to play, he'd often spend it with cousin Earl. Sometimes they would go fishing. If it was hot—which was pretty much every day in the summer—they'd cool off by swimming in one of the local ponds or creeks, the icy water washing away the heat as it chilled them to the bone. Other times they would play with some old beat-up plastic trucks and cars Earl owned, or they would take a couple of tires, climb inside, and roll down any hill they could find. Occasionally, they'd join other local kids for a game of tag or hide-and-seek.

"It was a funny thing about Elvis," Earl recalled. "He was really a cut-up kid, and when we were alone, he was just as outgoing and talkative as I was. But when we'd team up with other kids we knew, he would get very quiet and just kind of follow along, almost hanging back from the rest. Because he got so much taunting from the local kids, he automatically went into a shell, drawing back like a puppy waiting to be kicked, but always hoping to be accepted. Once he saw they weren't going to get on him, then he'd open up, join in, and let himself have fun."

But the camaraderie was usually short lived and, ultimately, resented by Elvis. "It would hurt and confuse Elvis that the same kids who'd root for him to score a touchdown would snicker at his family a month later in school," explained Greenwood. "So with every succeeding year, it took longer for him to open up, because it was harder for him to forget the comments he'd heard. The older he got, the shyer and more introverted he got."

Regardless of whom he was with, Elvis always needed to be home by dinnertime. For most families in the area, meals didn't vary much: corn bread, black-eyed peas, collard greens, potatoes, and grits. And if it was a good day at the pond, fish might be part of the meal. If it wasn't boiled, it was fried; but however prepared, there wasn't very much of it. There were very few chubby sharecroppers. Those who were, like Gladys, owed their extra weight to drinking or avoiding field work. Alcohol was cheap; food might be hard to come by, but one could always find a drink.

Elvis had been a round-faced and dough-bellied toddler, but he lost his baby fat by the time he was seven or eight. He grew into a thin adolescent and was downright skinny as a teenager and didn't really fill out until after he graduated from high school. Heredity had something to do with it—his father and J. D. had been thin men—but it also might have been that Elvis didn't have as much to eat as he should have. Considering the conditions he grew up under, it's miraculous that his health and teeth were as good as they were, which says a lot about Gladys making sure he was cared for.

To anyone visiting, Vernon and Gladys seemed like a typical couple. But a closer look showed that they were not a unit and lived very separate lives. They seldom addressed one another. On most nights after dinner, Vernon excused himself and left for parts unknown, and Gladys had long since stopped asking where. Her world revolved around whatever shack they currently occupied, and Vernon found every reason to be out of their home, even if it meant just sitting for hours on the front stoop. Other than at meal times or church, they were seldom together.

Their common denominator was Elvis, although they didn't see eye to eye there, either. If Vernon or Gladys came into some extra money, rather than spend it on something sensible like food or clothes, Gladys would buy something special for Elvis, trying to make up for their poverty. Vernon would want to tear his hair out at what he thought was a frivolous expense, but Gladys always got her way.

When Gladys decided Elvis should have a guitar, she skipped meals, made do with raggedy clothes, and scrimped and saved until she had enough money to buy Elvis the guitar—a gift that meant more to her at the time. He would have preferred a bicycle, but he knew better than to complain.

They went to the secondhand store and Gladys proudly counted out her accumulated change. The shop owner showed Elvis how to hold the guitar and how to strum it, while Gladys beamed with pride. From the time Elvis was born, Gladys dreamed of her son being a star, partly because as a young girl *she'd* wanted to be a performer. If she couldn't live out the dream, maybe, just maybe, she could live it through Elvis. It was a fantasy that kept her going. On his part, he knew one sure way to please his mother was to sing for her.

Despite his skepticism, once the guitar was his, Elvis grew to love his instrument. What little he could play he taught himself simply by experimenting. He'd sit alone for hours and try to play along with the radio, singing and strumming. When he wasn't plucking out a tune, he carried the guitar around almost constantly. After having spent his whole life doing without, he suddenly had something that few others had, and it made him feel special.

It was a tradition to listen to the Grand Ole Opry on the radio every Saturday night. Gladys, Vernon, and Elvis would go over to Tom Greenwood's house to hear the show. If there were a lot of people present, Elvis would sit off to the side and just listen. But if it was a small group, Elvis would start singing along, careful not to sing too loud and drown out the performers on the radio. Years later, he would admit he'd never really been a country music fan—he'd just liked singing.

Although music was becoming a passion, the young Elvis also enjoyed movies. To earn the admission price to the movie theater, he and his cousin would go out to the main road and search through the grass for discarded pop bottles, or they would look for an odd job to do for one of the neighbors. Most of the films were old by the time they reached Tupelo, but for Elvis, they were still a breath of fresh air. Even for the polite, seemingly mild-mannered Elvis, the reality of his world got to be too much, and movies took him away to another place.

Although Elvis became notorious for sudden, violent outbursts as an adult, he seldom displayed anger as a child. Nor did he get into trouble, having been raised with manners—and a deep-seated abhorrence of Gladys's displeasure. She could wound Elvis more with the pain of disappointment than a whipping stick ever would. Quite simply, he hated feeling that he had failed her.

But every now and then the temper he held inside would peek through. One day he was headed home from school and passed by a roadside fruit stand offering fresh-from-the-tree apples for sale. Elvis stopped to admire them, knowing how much Gladys loved apples. But he didn't have the nickel needed to buy one and started to walk away. Frustrated and tired of doing without, he snuck back and took one of the apples off the farmer's truck and ran all the way home. There had been so many, he reasoned, one wouldn't be missed, and there was no way the farmer would sell them all. If they were just going to go bad, why shouldn't he get one for his mother?

When Elvis proudly plopped down the apple in front of a very surprised Gladys, she was just as delighted as he'd hoped she'd be—until she asked what tree he had picked it from, and the guilt showed through on his face. She demanded to know where the apple came from, and when he told her, she flew into a sputtering rage.

"You *never* take something without paying unless it's a gift," she shouted at him. "You wanna end up in jail like your daddy someday?"

Elvis was frightened by the intensity of her reaction. He couldn't have known she was terrified of him getting a reputation in town as a thief, or turning out to be like Vernon. It was a child's silly mistake, but to Gladys it was an ominous portent of Elvis's following in the unfortunate footsteps of his father. She grabbed him by the shirt collar and led him out the door.

He begged her to stop, but no amount of crying and carrying on could sway Gladys. Curious neighbors peeked out their windows at the sounds of Elvis's pleas, and the humiliation made him so angry he cried out even more. He struggled, but Gladys had a grip of iron. She half-dragged Elvis back to the stand, her face blotched with fury. The farmer jumped up at the commotion, and Gladys planted Elvis directly in front of him.

Gladys held out the apple and made Elvis admit to stealing it and apologize. Elvis did, head hung in shame and crying. The farmer was a little taken aback by all the emotion. He thanked Gladys but also tried to tell her it was a case of boys will be boys, but she wasn't buying.

They walked back home in silence, Gladys's head held high, Elvis's chin digging a hole in his chest. When they reached the house, Gladys ordered Elvis to stay inside as punishment for what he'd done; then she left, partly to calm herself down, and partly to give Elvis a chance to think about what he'd done.

But he didn't make use of the timeout in quite the way she'd hoped. Shamed beyond words, frustrated that he had lacked a lousy nickel in the first place, and mortified that his mother was so disappointed in him, Elvis had a full-blown tantrum. He attacked the walls of their shack, peeling off the cheap wallpaper Gladys had put up in an attempt to make it homier. Elvis tore at the paper with a vengeance, wanting to rip everything about their life into pieces. He had ruined two walls and was midtear on the third when Gladys came back in and caught him.

For a split second, they stared at each other—Gladys with stunned surprise, Elvis with defiance. Then in a flash, Gladys scooped Elvis up and gave him the spanking of his life. In fact, it was the first and only spanking he ever got.

The only thing Elvis would say about the apple incident later in life is that none of it would have happened if they hadn't been so poor to begin with.

FIRST TASTE OF APPLAUSE

The biggest event of the year in Tupelo was the annual Alabama-Mississippi Fair. Kids looked forward to this almost as much as they did Christmas. The adults enjoyed it just as much. Men put on clean shirts and trousers, and women pressed their nicest dresses to go on rides and see livestock. The biggest attractions of the fair were the farm animal shows: best hogs, best cows, which cows gave the most milk, and hog calling, among others. Once you got away from the livestock end, the fair took on a wonderful aroma of chili cook-offs and baking contests.

For kids, the rides were what made the fair special. The cornerstone, of course, was the Ferris wheel, which creaked and jerked as it groaned through its revolutions, but Elvis and his cousins would happily wait in line an hour to ride on it. At the top, the flat farmland stretched out forever.

But the highlight of the fair for many people was the talent contest, and anyone with even the slightest bit of ability participated, from juggling to singing to playing the spoons. By the time Elvis was 10, his voice was developing into a thing of crystal beauty, and when the fair came to town that year, everybody in the family thought it would be a wonderful idea for Elvis to enter the talent contest.

Everybody but Elvis. Just the thought of standing in front of a crowd of strangers was too terrifying. Vernon tried to come to his son's aid, but Gladys was determined, telling Elvis it would make her so proud. He knew he really didn't have a choice, so he agreed to compete. The promise of free entry into the fair and a complimentary lunch made the decision easier to accept.

The day of the contest, Elvis was very nervous and distracted himself by obsessing over the clothes he'd wear. He tried on what few clothes he owned in every possible combination 10 times. Gladys was in a state of barely controlled mania, fluttering over him like a bustterfly, constantly smoothing his already-plastered-down hair, and adjusting his clothes. Elvis wore a jacket that was at least one size too small and pants that would have fallen off him without a belt. He clutched his worn guitar for dear life.

He was excited, nervous, anxious, and thrilled all at once. At one point, he told Gladys he was going to be sick. She made him sit with his head between his knees until he felt better. And this was before he even left the house.

When everyone got to the fair, the rest of the family scouted out seats while Gladys went backstage with Elvis. The tent was packed even though it must have been 100 degrees inside. People fanned themselves with pieces of paper and kept climbing over the packed rows of seats to go out and buy lemonade.

Backstage, Elvis silently mouthed the words to his song over and over while Gladys wet his hair for the hundredth time. He was terrified he would forget the words to the song and humiliate himself. After telling him she had never been more proud, Gladys gave him a final hug and left to go find her seat.

One of the contest officials patted Elvis on the shoulder and gave him some advice: "If you feel yourself getting scared, son, just close your eyes and pretend you're all alone. Or just pick out one person to sing to. Works every time."

Gladys settled in at her chair just as the first act was introduced. After what seemed like hours of countless poorly sung country songs, she spotted Elvis in the wings waiting to go on. He had a death grip on his guitar and a silly grin on his face, which was flushed a deep red. His adrenaline was pumping so hard he looked to be on the verge of hyperventilating.

When they announced his name, Elvis strode uncertainly toward center stage, which was nothing more than bare earth at the front of the tent. A friendly chorus of chuckles greeted him when he got to the microphone, because he was too small to reach it. One of the judges brought out a chair and told Elvis to stand on it so everybody could see him; then he retreated so Elvis could perform.

He stood there quietly for several moments, unmoving and almost frozen as he scanned the audience. His eyes grew big, then abruptly closed. After a few more tense seconds, during which Gladys looked as if she would faint, Elvis opened his eyes, put his guitar in playing position, strummed twice, and then warbled out Red Foley's "Old Shep," all the while looking straight into the first row. The song is a tearjerker about a boy and his dog, and a number of sniffles could be heard among the audience. Elvis had looked so small and vulnerable up there when he began but grew more secure as the song went on. By the end he was singing in a clear, strong voice, a cappella, since he forgot to strum the guitar after the first two times.

When he finished, the place erupted into an avalanche of applause. The sudden noise scared him at first, but then Elvis broke into a big smile before leaving the stage. Luckily, he was one of the last acts, so he didn't have to wait long for the judging.

The officials brought all the contestants back on stage to announce the winners. Gladys grabbed Vernon's arm in between wiping away her flood of tears. To Elvis's surprise and to the screaming and cheering of his family, he won second place and walked off with five dollars in prize money.

After a final bow from the winners, the contest was over, and Elvis ran to meet his family, eyes almost wild with happiness and shock. He was literally hopping with excitement. Without any hesitation, he turned his five-dollar winnings over to Gladys, which made her cry even harder.

While it may have been the happiest day in Gladys's life to that point, it was also a turning point for Elvis. It was his first taste of public approval, and he was almost drunk with the unaccustomed feeling of affection and acceptance. For the rest of the day, the smile never left his face, and Gladys couldn't stop hugging him. Elvis even returned Vernon's hug, all was so right with the world.

For that day, at least, Elvis was the object of everyone's congratulations and good wishes, instead of their scorn and ridicule. By singing a song, he had been accepted, even if only for that moment. The next morning, it was just a sweet memory; nothing had changed, except perhaps inside

Elvis. But it was enough to set the ball in motion. It was enough to instill in his mind that singing equals love, and love equals acceptance. Elvis would seek that sensation of approval and public love for most of his life. No matter how famous he got or how successful his career, every time he set foot on a stage, he was still a little boy seeking love and acceptance, trying to shuck off a hundred years' worth of family shame.

Chapter 4

THE ROAD TO MEMPHIS

Like many American cities, Tupelo as a whole enjoyed an economic boost in the years following the end of World War II. But for the sharecroppers and other poor families, life went on with frustrating sameness. From where Elvis sat in late 1948, as the dirt swirled in the winter wind across the barren fields, the coming year seemed indistinguishable from the ones preceding it. So nothing could have prepared Elvis—or his parents—for what would be a year of abrupt change, renewed hope, and dashed expectations.

Although only in her thirties, Gladys moved like someone twice her age. Poor nutrition combined with her increased drinking had taken a sharp physical toll. Most days found Gladys hung over and suffering from nausea and splitting headaches. The official family line, though, had her battling lingering flu or suffering from female troubles.

Vernon took Gladys's ailments calmly, seeing them for what they were, but Elvis fretted constantly, terrified his mother might die and leave him to fend for himself. Gladys was more than his anchor and the person who loved him more than anyone; he believed he was born to care for her. If she were gone, he might as well be, too.

When Elvis entered his teens, he was known as being shy and eccentric. When everyone else wore crew cuts, Elvis boasted long, flowing blonde hair that fell almost to his shoulders. But such expressions of stubborn individuality meant he was often treated as an outcast by schoolmates. Some of the boys in school called him Miss Elvis, but he ignored it; not caring what they said showed that they couldn't hurt him and showed that fitting in wasn't important to him—even though he was desperate for that acceptance. But since they didn't like him anyway, he figured he might as well do what *he* liked, and he liked his hair long. So did Gladys.

Vernon didn't, but that was of no consequence to Elvis. While he was cordial and respectful to his father, he felt no warmth or strong emotional bonds. Unfortunately, like most men of his era, Vernon had been raised to keep a lid on his feelings and take things as they come. So the gulf between father and child deepened, and Elvis interpreted Vernon's self-containment as a lack of true caring. As he got older, Elvis began to resent his father for being content to scrape by. They were constantly changing shacks but never improving their living conditions.

Perhaps most confusing and frustrating to Elvis was that it was still his responsibility to be the man of the house, a notion Gladys had instilled in him since Vernon had gone to prison. He wasn't allowed to be mad ssat Vernon, but it was okay to do his work for him, as it were. He was angry at so much but swallowed his feelings, lest he rage at his father. Anger wasn't proper, and he couldn't bear the thought of giving Gladys another reason to be disappointed in him.

Added to that was Elvis's own guilt for being too slight to work in the fields, for being the only one there to help, and for just being help-less to help enough. He took any legitimate opportunity he had to make some extra money to help out, even if it meant getting up at four in the morning to deliver milk before school. Between working, helping Gladys at home, and going to school, about the only free time Elvis had was Sundays after church, when he would often spend the day just wandering the countryside.

He loved the sights and smells of the country and felt recharged after spending the day in its embrace. There wasn't much to see on these treks except for soybean and cotton fields, until the day Elvis stumbled upon a new world that moved his imagination and stirred his soul.

Like the rest of the South, Tupelo was segregated; the black section was so far out of town as to not be part of it at all. In fact, the only time blacks mingled with whites was at the Alabama-Mississippi Fair when it came to town. Even then, each group stayed to itself, as was the custom.

One day, Elvis found himself in the black section, which, if possible, was even poorer and more rundown than the poorest white section in Tupelo. A couple of bent old men were tending a wilted-looking garden, and a few women and children gave him curious looks as he walked by. He came across a man sitting on his porch, softly singing a gospel song, which stirred something in Elvis.

The following Sunday, Elvis dragged Earl out to the black section of town, where they watched a black church service by peeking in through the windows. When the congregation rose to sing a hymn, Elvis sat on the ground, his back against the outside wall. His eyes were closed, and his knees kept time to the music. "Don't it sound like how heaven's gotta be?" he asked Earl, "relaxing and peaceful, with no more hurt."

Elvis made the trip to that little church on the outskirts of town regularly after that until he and his family moved away, but he never told his mother where he went. While he felt increasingly responsible for Gladys, at the same time Elvis was less apt to stay home and keep her company, even when she made it clear that's what she wanted. The inner conflict between wanting to take care of his mother, wishing it wasn't all up to him, and needing to take care of his own needs had already started a juggling act that would permanently retard his emotional development and undermine his independence.

Not only did Gladys depend on her son to love her unconditionally, she also leaned on him emotionally. But while she may have felt better sharing her burdens, they weighed heavily on the young Elvis, especially when she would fret—usually after a fight with Vernon—that they might have to move away from Tupelo in order for Vernon to find work. Vernon had no intention of leaving his hometown, but in the end he'd have no choice.

Most sharecroppers liked to drink, but liquor was illegal. And because most couldn't afford to pay for good liquor on the black market, they simply made their own. That was illegal, too, but the local authorities usually turned a blind eye to moonshine made for personal consumption. But their sight suddenly improved if there was an attempt to turn it into a business, as Vernon did.

On a chokingly hot summer day, the local sheriff came knocking on Tom Greenwood's door. He announced Vernon Presley had been arrested for running an illegal distillery, so they had to check out the homes of his known associates. Later that day, Gladys and Elvis showed up at the Greenwoods' looking ashen and grim, Gladys's eyes swollen and red from crying.

Gladys tearfully told them how the sheriff had taken Vernon away to the local jail in broad daylight for everyone to see. "They took him away in handcuffs like a common criminal for the world to see," she wailed. "How could they be so cruel to Elvis? How could *he* be so stupid? Why'd he do this to us again? Wasn't the first time enough?"

But she also said the sheriff gave Vernon a choice—either stand trial to face a sure conviction or leave Tupelo and never come back.

Tom Greenwood suggested they go to Memphis. He had already decided to sell the land and dairy in Tupelo and use that money to buy a couple of gas stations in Memphis. He even promised Gladys he'd hire Vernon to work at one of the stations. "Memphis is as good a city as any," Tom told her. "And at least there you'll have family."

Vernon was released the next morning and given a couple of weeks to get his affairs in order. As their time in Tupelo wound down, Elvis suffered through conflicting feelings about the move. While he was eager to get away from the stares and disapproval of their neighbors, the thought of moving to a strange place scared him. Life in Tupelo might be horrible, but it was familiar.

As moving day approached, his family's spirits were surprisingly high. Gladys had come to see Vernon's arrest as a blessing in disguise. He had begged her forgiveness and promised to get a steady job and take better care of his family. It gave Gladys hope and convinced her that Memphis would be a fresh start. Things *had* to be better for them there, and that gave Gladys a sense of anticipation. And anything that made his mother happy, made Elvis happy.

Had the Greenwoods not been on their way to Memphis, who knows where Vernon would have taken his family, and who knows if Elvis would have ever gotten the chance to sing. The mysterious way life works out fascinated Elvis as he got older, and he could only come to one conclusion: "Jesse's hand was guiding us."

Ben staked Vernon $150 so he could buy a beat-up 1939 Plymouth for the trip and have some cash to help him get settled once in Memphis. Moving day for the Presleys came in mid-August. What little packing there was to be done took only a few minutes. Gladys simply took a large cardboard box and filled it with all their belongings. There was room to spare.

She stood in her empty shack, suddenly emotional at leaving. But Elvis, eager to leave, shed no tears. As their car pulled away, Elvis looked back through the window for a final look, and then turned around to watch the road to Memphis, clutching his guitar the whole way.

It was a long, bumpy four-hour drive. While Vernon and Gladys sat in their respective silences, Elvis strummed his guitar and watched the landscape change from rural to urban the closer they got to their destination. Cotton fields gave way to industrial smokestacks spewing bad-smelling fumes, and the road became crowded with cars.

Having no specific destination, Vernon drove to downtown Memphis. In the heart of the city, prosperity and enthusiasm surrounded them. Every other car they passed was shiny and new. Clean, shop-lined streets were filled with men in suits and women in fashionable dresses and matching hats. Unlike sharecroppers, who trudged their way through life, these city folk walked with a spring in their step. Even breathing was easier, the air free of choking dust. As he watched the purposeful movement and felt the energy, Elvis dared to feel optimistic. Maybe his mother was right. Maybe Memphis *was* a promised land of opportunity.

After splurging on a lunch of cheeseburgers, fries, and milkshakes, Vernon set out to find his family a place to live. At first they were awestruck at the stylish houses nestled on neatly manicured streets; the thought of living in such splendor made them dizzy. But their high hopes were rudely dashed by harsh financial realities. The neighborhoods that most appealed to them were far beyond their means. By nightfall, they were fighting crushing discouragement, and a shroud of despair settled on Elvis.

In Tupelo, only a privileged few didn't have to work in the fields, and even those who owned small plots of their own weren't *that* much better off. Someone really well off, like Orville Bean, was easily despised and dismissed. But mostly, whatever their bank accounts, they were all simple farmers with dirt under their nails. Memphis was different. Being so close to the good life made being poor even more unbearable, and Elvis felt more an outcast and more hopeless than ever.

They ate a dinner of peanut butter and banana sandwiches Gladys had brought along, and then parked on a deserted street to sleep. Elvis lay awake most of the night, unable to sleep in the unfamiliar surroundings with the strange city sounds. In the dark, Elvis was suddenly aware how close they were to being homeless, especially now in a new city with no relations. Frightened by their uncertain future, he cried himself to sleep before dawn, and he never lost the fear of being on the street with nowhere to go.

The next day, they finally found an apartment they could afford, at 572 Poplar Avenue. It was a boxlike, single-room, furnished apartment in an industrial part of town. They unpacked what few belongings they had and tried to adjust to their new home.

The little apartment was dark and depressing, with small, dirty windows that barely opened wide enough to let air in. There was a communal bathroom on their floor that they would share with five other families.

Elvis spent those first weeks in a daze. Nothing put him at ease. While it was true their new apartment was nicer than the shacks they'd lived in before, it didn't feel like a home. In Tupelo, Elvis had always been able to escape outdoors and feel free in the open flatland, or clear his head with the sweet, heavy smell of a summer night. Now, instead of a front yard, there was a concrete sidewalk and a busy street clouded by exhaust fumes and the acrid discharge of nearby factories. No more lying on the grass watching the sun set over lazy farmland; they were surrounded by the ugliness of city industry.

Scenery aside, Elvis missed the sense of community he had previously taken for granted. The Presleys had hardly been the favorites of East Tupelo, but at least there Elvis had known who his neighbors were. City people seemed happier to keep to themselves.

Of course, that suited Vernon and Gladys just fine—no nosy neighbors asking embarrassing questions. But it also meant they were more isolated than ever, especially Elvis.

As soon as the Greenwoods arrived in Memphis, Elvis went over to visit. "I came running when my mom called that Elvis was there," Earl recalled, "then stopped dead in my tracks when I saw him. His blonde hair was gone, replaced by jet black, lacquered locks. He could have hit a truck head-on and survived." He was also sporting mascara to cover his blonde lashes.

His new fashion statement was both an opportunity to reinvent himself and a ploy to garner attention. Even if he still ended up an outsider in high school, Elvis was determined not to be invisible.

Their determination to see Elvis educated was Vernon and Gladys's one shared passion, and it had set them apart from most of the other share-croppers who thought kids needed to know only the basics of "readin', writin', and 'rithmetic" before going to work in the fields full time. The Presleys were among the minority who believed a high school diploma guaranteed a better life, so it was serious business.

With Gladys feeling "under the weather," it was Vernon who accompanied Elvis on his first day. After registration, the students were directed to their first class, so Vernon waved goodbye to his son and headed home. No sooner had he walked through the door than Elvis returned home, too. "I shut the door behind me only to hear it open right back up," Vernon would relate later. "In walks Elvis, saying it'd be better if he went job hunting instead of staying in school."

Gladys bolted out of bed and ordered him back to class. Elvis pleaded his case, claiming the school was too big and he couldn't find his way around. The mere size of Humes High, with 1,500 students, had terrified him. To someone used to sparsely populated country schools, it seemed bigger than all of Tupelo. But Gladys was unmoved and over wails of protest marched him back to school. This time he stayed, probably out of fear that if he didn't, Gladys would sit right there in the class with him to make sure he did.

Elvis was an average student at best and floated on the fringe. He wanted to try out for football, but to his bitter disappointment, Gladys wouldn't hear of it. She was too afraid he might get hurt—a somewhat ironic stand since the neighborhood they lived in had a rough, city feel to it and wasn't a particularly safe place to walk around in alone at night.

Despite Tom Greenwood's offer of a job, Vernon never took him up on it. As 1948 drew to a close, the combined Presley income was about $35 a week. Gladys occasionally found work in a factory, although it seldom lasted more than a couple of days, and Vernon sometimes drove a truck for a wholesale food company. Elvis now contributed to the family earnings by spending weekends and afternoons after school offering his services to mow lawns, clean out gutters, or do anything else someone in the neighborhoods that could afford such help might want done.

Although they were making more money than they had in Tupelo, it cost more to live in Memphis, so the family was still swimming upstream and in over their heads. Despite having been in Memphis for just a few months, the Presleys found that their dreams of a new way of life were all but dead. Memphis was supposed to have been a new beginning, but nothing had changed except their address.

The disappointment hit Gladys the hardest. Her frustration at their inability to improve their standard of living drove her even more to drink. Bloated and aging rapidly, Gladys had outbursts of despair and rage toward Vernon, unlocked by the key of liquor. She covered the same ground time after time: no food, bills and rent due or past due, no steady job, Vernon not trying hard enough . . . it was an ongoing mantra.

Elvis's resentment of Vernon soared, and his determination to somehow rescue his mother from her torment stiffened. He daydreamed about getting her all the things she had gone without: a washing machine, decent clothes, new shoes ... but for now, he had to settle with merely helping to keep them from being evicted. His efforts to help the family meant his studies suffered. He got a job delivering papers and had to get up so early that in the afternoon he couldn't keep his eyes open and was frequently reprimanded for falling asleep in class.

His frustration grew as he saw classmates after school playing touch football or leisurely walking home, homework their biggest concern. He *might* get to do homework, if he wasn't too exhausted after working at whatever job he currently had. In Tupelo, where more children his age worked in the fields than attended school, there wasn't so much a reminder of what he was missing as there was in Memphis. Elvis's anger was always indirect. He'd slam doors and punch walls, bust out windows of deserted tenement buildings with rocks, or just run as fast as he could down the streets until he wore himself out. Or he'd turn inward and sit with his guitar for hours, shutting the world out. At no time did he ever say a word to Vernon about it directly—not then, not later.

In the spring of 1949, the Presleys were in desperate straits. Their car had broken down, they couldn't afford to get it fixed, and they were behind in rent and afraid of being kicked out on the street. Vernon and Gladys were forced to swallow their pride and apply for welfare. Elvis was so shamed by their desperation, he didn't want any of their relatives to know.

Their caseworker from the Memphis Housing Authority was a Mrs. Richardson, who came to interview Vernon and Gladys to determine if they qualified for assistance. When he read the report years later, Elvis was stunned to learn that Vernon was sending $10 a month to Miss Minnie, Elvis's grandmother, in West Point, Mississippi. While his wife and son were going without, he was secretly helping support his own mother. Ironically, he and Elvis might have been more alike than either guessed.

That Elvis obtained a copy of that report shows how deep an impression going on welfare had made on him. Like people who display their first dollar to show how far they've come in life, Elvis kept the report as a haunting reminder of where he'd been—and where he feared he might someday return.

In May 1949, right before Elvis finished his freshman year at Humes High, the Presleys moved to 185 Winchester Street in the Lauderdale Courts, a government housing project. Even though the project itself was in need of repairs, their new apartment was like a dream come true for Vernon, Gladys, and Elvis. There were two bedrooms, a separate kitchenette, and a private bathroom. It was the most luxurious place they had ever lived in, and for now, they were as proud as if they had just bought a house.

Elvis's pride was short lived. During the last week of school, Elvis overheard a cutting remark and the accompanying laughter from some girls in his history class about Elvis living with the "coloreds in the projects." The apartment complex where the city relocated them was integrated and mostly black. The Presleys had been so relieved and so happy with the comparative luxury that they hadn't paid much attention to who their neighbors were. But in the South during the forties and fifties, racial discrimination was alive and well and considered socially acceptable. It *was* a stigma to live "with coloreds."

A few days after Elvis overheard the two girls, a swaggering bully walked by and called him "so weird only the niggers will let you live near 'em," adding, "Don' get too close—who knows what we'll catch."

Elvis squeezed his eyes shut so tight he saw yellow flashes. All the frustration and rage, bottled up since he first heard taunts while still a toddler, exploded to the surface and let loose. Elvis turned and landed a direct punch on the side of the boy's head. It ended up being more a scuffle than a real fight. The other boy's friends broke it up, and when the dust cleared, it was Elvis who emerged with hardly a scratch, while the boy's nose and lip dripped blood.

There was a surprised silence among the students. Because Elvis was so shy, people had made the mistake of thinking he was a pushover. And maybe up to that moment he had been, but now he was old enough and tired enough to try to put an end to the verbal abuse and silence his tormentors. It was a turning point and also a painful lesson. Even if punches could keep words from being spoken, they couldn't force people to like and accept you.

Chapter 5

FIRST LOVE

Elvis was cautiously optimistic as he began his sophomore year at Humes. He had become more confident and planned to enjoy school and participate in activities. Elvis also wanted more independence, which meant gently weaning himself from his mother's tendency to coddle him, such as her insistence that she walk him to school. The first time he told her he'd rather walk by himself, she threw herself on the floor weeping. Eventually, she agreed to a compromise, and for the rest of his sophomore year, whenever Gladys wanted to walk him to school, she did—but from at least a block behind.

Unfortunately, Elvis's efforts to join the football team were not as successful. After getting permission from Vernon to try out, he went to sign up during the first week of school. The coach was standing nearby and announced that before Elvis could even try out, he had to cut his hair. This, of course, was not an option.

Rather than get depressed, Elvis found other interests. He liked shop class and joined the Reserve Officer's Training Corps (ROTC), where he learned to love the precision drills and military talk. After he became famous, Elvis went back to Humes and donated enough money so that the ROTC drill team could buy brand-new uniforms, partially out of appreciation for their letting him participate.

Academically, Elvis still struggled. His best subject in school was English; his worst were math and history. Part of his problem was that both math and history required a lot of homework time, which he simply didn't have. That fall, Elvis was hired as an usher at Loew's State movie theater in downtown Memphis. He worked from five to ten each night and earned $12.75 a week. He gave most of his paycheck to Gladys, but always saved a little for himself in a secret stash fund to buy clothes or a cheeseburger and fries after school. But eventually he was forced to quit the job when his grades began falling and teachers again complained that he was sleeping through class.

A year later, during his junior year, school officials stepped in yet again when they discovered Elvis was working a full-shift job from three to eleven while both his parents were unemployed. Elvis's counselor sent Vernon and Gladys a letter requesting a meeting, where they were told Elvis was carrying too heavy a load and they had to make a decision: it was either work or school.

Although Elvis liked having money in his pocket, he was relieved to have more free time. Now 16, he had an interest in girls that was reaching a fever pitch. Although Elvis was still thin, he was filling out and growing into his features. Even though his speech and grammar were still rough, his voice was changing and gaining a silky resonance that he was learning to use to its full advantage.

Elvis enjoyed shopping and loved browsing through racks of old and out-of-date shirts, jackets, and pants at thrift shops and secondhand stores. It didn't matter if there were a few holes or tears, because Gladys was still a whiz with a needle and thread. His wardrobe reflected a style that was as startling as his hair: pink shirts matched with green pants and a striped jacket, plaids and polka dots freely mixed. But somehow, it worked for him.

Elvis was aware that not everyone shared his taste, but he shrugged it off, joking, "At least it'll be easy to spot me if I ever get run over." He felt good about his choices and loved it when he saw people do a double take as he walked by. Elvis's desire to belong hadn't diminished—he just wanted to belong on his terms, with his own style.

His sudden rush of independence rattled Gladys but not as much as his interest in girls would. Elvis had a tendency to like well-dressed, blonde, pretty girls, but claimed only their "goodness" attracted his interest. It was apparently just coincidence that the sweetest girls he saw also happened to be the prettiest. Elvis's hormones kicked into high gear the summer before junior year when he was rehired by the Loew's State movie theater and became smitten with a candy-counter girl named Sue.

There had been crushes before, but they'd been confined to stolen glances and wishful thinking. Sue's blonde hair and sparkling green eyes consumed Elvis's thoughts and ignited his fantasies. He was also paralyzed with fear. Most teenagers are shy and awkward, but Elvis took it to new heights. He was poor, living in the projects, and embarrassed about it.

Plus, he considered his body awkward and face ugly and assumed any girl would think him homely.

But Sue stirred his dormant sexuality to such a degree that he went out of his way to introduce himself and talk to her. Unfortunately, their potential romance met an untimely demise after Elvis was fired for fighting with another usher who he claimed was bad-mouthing him to Sue. "I didn't mean to hit him," Elvis explained to Earl. "But he made me mad. I did it before I knew what I was doing."

Once Elvis finally got up the courage to ask his first girl out, he was surprised it was so easy. Her name was Louanne, and they went to a movie. But Elvis soon learned the downside of dating—there aren't always fireworks.

So he set out to find his next companion and became single-minded in his pursuit of a Saturday-night date. Through sheer doggedness, more often than not, he found one. The faces changed on a regular basis, but not his dating routine. Elvis would take the girl to a movie, stop at the local diner afterward for a cheeseburger, and then take her home. He seldom saw the same girl more than once or twice. But with each date, he built up a little more confidence, and he kept on asking, hoping to find the girl he'd want to call his own.

Elvis lustily eyed the rich, cultured girls with their perfumed skin and comfortable lifestyles. Some would look back, snared by Elvis's brooding looks. Startled by their attention, Elvis quickly melted into the background, knowing he was out of their league and resenting them for it. He explained his professed disinterest by claiming he was looking for a girl who was pure, innocent, and simple.

His view of women even at that young age was based on a double standard. A woman who was good, simple, and pure did not exhibit sexual desire and passion, and she certainly didn't have any prior sexual experience—an ideal with little basis in reality. Sexually, Elvis would develop into a young man alternately repressed and obsessed, with a fair share of issues. Sex became more a weapon than a tool of love, and from the beginning of his life, it represented conflicting meanings and emotions.

As an infant and toddler, Elvis shared his parents' bed. Later when he moved to the couch of the one-room shack, he was still privy to their sexual relationship. Despite Gladys's emotional distance and estrangement from Vernon, she still enjoyed sex with her husband and, until liquor doused her passion, pursued it with gusto.

According to Agnes Greenwood, one of Gladys's favorite stories was the time Elvis attacked Vernon after he'd been released from jail. "I guess we was getting carried away making noise, and Elvis comes running over, hitting Vernon's backside, telling him to stop hurting his mama. Oh, my two men fighting over me," Gladys laughed, oblivious to the trauma such an event would cause her son.

After that, Vernon and Gladys tried to be quiet, but their creaky bed didn't always cooperate, and Gladys would regale Agnes with another risqué tale. "Last night we were, you know, romancing, and sure enough, Elvis wakes up like a bolt, wanting to know if I'm okay—he thought I'd cried in pain. Well, Vernon didn't want his rump bruised again, so he just froze 'til we could hear Elvis was back asleep. But we stayed that way so long, Vernon got a cramp in a most painful spot," Gladys said, giggling like a schoolgirl. "I told Vernon he's gonna have to explain to Elvis about the birds and bees before he suffers a serious injury."

Thousands of youngsters before and after Elvis have been exposed to their parents' sexual relationship—especially in poor families living in houses so small that privacy is nonexistent. But his confusion arose because instead of turning to Vernon after their act of physical intimacy, she'd turn to her young son for emotional intimacy, and it set son against father on the most primitive of levels.

When Elvis was a toddler sharing Gladys's bed while Vernon was locked up, Gladys told him he was her little man. Not only was Elvis Gladys's son, she also made it clear he was a kind of mate. When Vernon returned, he took back what Elvis thought was his rightful place, and the little boy felt an intense rivalry and jealousy. So the sounds of pleasure were interpreted as pain. Recalling it later stirred budding desires, forbidden fruit buried beneath a mountain of repressed guilt.

While this classic Oedipal confrontation played itself deep in Elvis's subconscious, Gladys complicated matters further by adding her own suffocating possessiveness and jealousy. Like many mothers, she felt no girl would ever be good enough for her son, but it went beyond that.

Elvis was aware that Gladys was cool toward the idea of his dating. She didn't have a life of her own and resented anybody or anything that took Elvis's time and attention away from her. She let him know he was all she had, all she would ever have. Gladys would get terribly agitated that he preferred another female's company over hers and found reasons for him not to go out. To his credit, Elvis stubbornly kept his plans—but only after Gladys managed to make him feel terrible that he was failing her. Elvis learned to keep the peace by either lying or not telling her he had a date until he was literally walking out the door.

The first girl who stole Elvis's heart was named Dixie Locke. They sat across the aisle from one another in English class during the final semester of his junior year and quickly struck up a friendly rapport. Interestingly, in that same class was Red West, an individual who would later play a prominent role in Elvis's life, but at the time they were barely casual acquaintances.

Smitten, Elvis asked Dixie out for a Pepsi after school. One date later, he fell hard and fast. Dixie was the girl of his dreams: pretty, petite, and blonde—a direct contrast to Gladys. To Elvis, she was the sweetest girl he'd ever talked to, with a soft voice and sparkling eyes. Dixie was quiet but more watchful than shy. Elvis sensed a familiar vulnerability in her, and that drew them together.

Dixie's girlfriends teased her about Elvis's choice of clothes and his dyed hair, but she ignored them or laughed about it. "I'm glad he's not like all the other boys," she once said. "He's got a mind of his own. I hate it when guys are like a pack of dogs chasing after the head mongrel, don't you? Besides, I think his hair is cute."

Elvis and Dixie frequently double-dated with Earl and his girlfriend Karen. Being underage meant their entertainment options were limited to going to movies, dining out in restaurants, or cruising in the beat-up old Plymouth that Elvis had bought for $35 as junk and fixed up himself. He had squirreled away money from his various jobs for two years in order to buy a car, which became his pride. Even then, big cars made him feel special.

During the time they were together, Dixie helped Elvis come out of his shell in a number of ways. First, just having a steady, pretty girlfriend who cared for him, accepted him, and found him attractive did wonders for Elvis's confidence. Elvis was happier and more himself around Dixie than with any girl before—and some have said since. There was a bounce in his step and he began to see the world in brighter colors at her side. Dixie was also an upbeat girl with a sly sense of humor who craftily maneuvered Elvis into being more open in groups.

Elvis was still very much the gentleman, but Dixie brought out a sensuality and sexuality in him that had more to do with an increased sense of self-confidence than any physical activity between them. He was still a virgin, and part of him desperately wanted to sleep with Dixie, but he'd felt too guilty to even suggest it until they were married, or at least engaged. Plus, if he asked and she said yes, that would tarnish her image of being good, simple, and pure. Beyond that, Gladys still exerted a strong influence on Elvis and warned him repeatedly that if he ever got a girl pregnant it would out and out kill her.

So their physical relationship was limited to kissing and light petting, but it was the most pleasure he'd ever experienced. The problem of privacy was solved by the Plymouth. They'd park on a quiet road on the outskirts of town, where the stars weren't dimmed by the city lights. They'd climb into the back and press close together or sit on the hood, while Elvis sang love songs to her for hours at a time. It was in this pure, rather rustic setting that Elvis first told Dixie he loved her.

Elvis was very emotional and impulsive, and confused crushes or sexual attraction for love throughout his life. But Dixie was his genuine first love. Elvis knew she was the one after he tearfully confessed to her that his family was still living in the projects on assistance, and her response was to hold him and gently rock him. If she accepted that, he thought, she surely loved him. He was mad for her and began to talk in terms of their future together.

His feelings for Dixie were not lost on Gladys, who tensed whenever Dixie's name was mentioned. The depth of Elvis's love was made clear when he told his mother he'd like to have Dixie over for dinner. Elvis had never invited anyone to their apartment before, and Gladys felt threatened. The dinner never happened, but Elvis did bring Dixie by to meet his parents after going to a movie one night.

To Elvis's dismay, Gladys, whom he expected to be embracing, was aloof and haughty. Vernon turned on the charm and made Dixie feel completely welcome. But instead of appreciating his dad's efforts, Elvis was furious, suspecting Vernon had been hitting on Dixie. But he calmed down after Dixie told him how much she liked Vernon and that Elvis must have inherited his sense of humor. The idea that Elvis shared any trait with Vernon stopped him short—and made him think all women were just a little crazy.

ANOTHER COMPETITION

Every year, Humes High sponsored a senior class variety show. It was a big event, one of the most anticipated of the whole term. The students who participated were stars for the week, and the winner's picture was posted for the remainder of the semester. After a lot of prodding and cajoling from Dixie, Elvis finally agreed to participate.

There were approximately 30 acts scheduled, and before the show started, everyone was told that whoever got the most applause would be the winner and get to do an encore. That night when Elvis took the stage, everyone there saw the potential of his power and charisma. At first he was the little boy back at the fair, self-conscious and gripping his guitar. But once he got into the song, he was transformed, and the audience couldn't take their eyes off him.

Loud clothes and coiffed hair aside, Elvis displayed a brooding animal magnetism in front of the student body that night that had most of the girls squirming. He fed off the crowd, and his sexuality percolated with the mutual heat. At that moment he could have had almost any girl—and a few of the guys—who stood spellbound.

To nobody's surprise, Elvis got the most applause. He was proud of himself and surprised by the power he had felt. The same rush he experienced at the fair came back, only it was more intense.

"They like me," he said, breathless but focused, when he came off stage. "They want me. I get to go up and sing again."

"Don't just stand here, go do it." Dixie gave him an impassioned kiss and pushed him toward the stage.

For the second time in his life, Elvis felt loved and accepted by the world at large through the simple use of his God-given voice.

One of Elvis's favorite pastimes was cruising along Beale Street, famous for its blues clubs and the heart of the Memphis "sound." During the day, when the clubs were dark, aspiring black musicians gathered on the sidewalks to play and sing. Elvis would pull his car to the curb and listen in rapt appreciation, quietly singing along but too respectful to let himself be heard. Beale Street was a beacon for aspiring singers, and Elvis was similarly drawn. Feeding off the energy of the street's history, Elvis began to believe that he would one day belong with the singers and musicians he listened to.

The fantasy of following in the footsteps of a Carl Perkins or a Hank Williams had helped Elvis survive years of barely livable conditions. But what started as an escape took on a life of its own. After thinking and dreaming about it for so long, he felt the dream become more and more of a real possibility in his mind as time wore on, but he had hesitated to talk about it to many people. Now there was no reason to be ashamed or feel silly—the variety show triumph brought Elvis's dreams of being a singer into the open.

But Elvis was two people: one wanted fame and adventure; the other wanted to get married, settle down, and have a family. Realistically, a person couldn't hit the road singing and be settled at the same time, but Elvis seldom let reality get in the way of his plans. With Dixie, he swam in newfound feelings and a self-confidence that was so out of character as to be awe inspiring. Elvis felt invincible and capable of doing it all. He was going to be a singer, and he was going to have Dixie for his very own—forever. He decided to propose on their prom night. It was going to be perfect.

Elvis had it all worked out. He stunned his cousin by detailing his plans. "I wanna have kids right away. Until my singing gets going, I'll work nights somewhere. Dixie'll move into my room, and we'll all live together. That way I can take care of both Mama and Dixie." The only thing he missed was asking Dixie what she thought, but he was convinced they shared one heart and one mind when it came to their love.

With Elvis looking toward a future with Dixie, he spent less time worrying about his parents' present situation. He started keeping more money for himself, which gradually put increased pressure on his parents to shoulder a greater share of the financial burden. Vernon in particular felt the added weight—Gladys had once again taken to her bed with an extended series of mysterious ailments, leaving him to take up the slack. Both Vernon and Gladys were so used to depending on Elvis to help bail them out, it never occurred to them he had been holding back.

Typically, Elvis was torn; he felt guilty about not helping out as much as he had in the past, but he wanted the freedom to take Dixie to a movie, or to fix his car, or even to save up for an engagement ring. He was desperate to simply luxuriate in his passion and resented any intrusion—even from his beloved mother. He was so wrapped up in his own world he pretended not to see his family slipping back into a familiar hole.

In the winter of 1952, when Vernon's claim of a bad back forced him to quit his job, the Presleys fell behind in the rent and were past due on their utilities. The Memphis Housing Authority wasted no time in sending a notice announcing they were delinquent more than $30 and in danger of losing the apartment. Gladys pulled it together and returned to work at St. Joseph's as a nurse's aide, but her take-home income pushed them over the city's poverty level, jeopardizing their welfare status. This had happened once before, and their options were simple: lose the extra income and "improved" financial status in order to keep the subsidized apartment, or keep the job and look for a new place to live. Previously, they had elected to keep the apartment, but this time Vernon and Gladys decided to move to a smaller, nonfunded apartment.

Their new home was closer into the city—less industrial, more urban. Developers had divided a house into cramped apartments that were even more depressing than their place in the projects. Elvis went back to sleeping on the lumpy couch, where he would lie awake in the dark, trying to plan a course of action that would satisfy Dixie, Gladys, and his dreams. He was angry they had moved to this tiny, mildew-smelling apartment, but he held his feelings inside.

He resented Gladys's coolness toward Dixie and her refusal to accept the girl as family. He also felt guilty at harboring animosity toward his mother, but instead of expressing his displeasure, he kept quiet and played the loving son doubly hard, while deep inside, his anger simmered like bubbling stew.

But he wasn't going to let his mother deter him from going to the senior prom. It was the event of the school year for the graduating class, and Elvis wanted to be a part of it. He'd been saving his money by sacrificing cheeseburgers and even a thrift-shop bargain or two in order to have enough for the tickets, tuxedo, and fancy dinner. Between his excitement and his nerves, he was bouncing off the walls as prom day neared.

A week before the dance, Elvis went to pick out his tux from a store on Beale Street. He chose a white tux with a white shirt and a white cummerbund, which would make his shock of black hair stand out even more—but made him self-conscious. "I feel like a waiter or something," he muttered.

But when he tried it on, he was transformed from a slender, gangly youth into a surprisingly dashing young man. Part of the transformation was simply seeing himself in clothes that fit perfectly. Preening like a parrot, he studied every angle of his reflection in the mirror. He felt so good about himself that his cheeks glowed with exhilaration.

Elvis was determined to do everything just right, and it's ironic that one of the things giving him the most jitters was the prospect of dancing in public.

The night of the prom, Gladys's eyes filled with tears when Elvis stepped out of the bathroom dressed in formal white down to his new buckskin shoes. She held a wadded-up handkerchief to her face, swallowing back rhythmic sobs. His intense focus on this night out with Dixie had made Gladys feel neglected, and sips from the bottle hidden in her robe added fuel to her emotional fire.

"Soon you'll be leaving your mama all alone to live your own life some-where," she wailed, having worked herself into a full head of steam. Elvis walked over and hugged her, although an edge of irritation hardened his smooth-shaven jaw. Still, he managed to calm her down enough so he felt okay to leave. He said goodnight and put Gladys and everything else out of his mind because tonight was going to be the most important night of his life.

Chapter 6

CHASING THE DREAM

For several days following the prom, Elvis dropped out of sight. He was already gone by the time Gladys woke up and still out when she went to bed. Even Earl Greenwood began to worry.

"I hadn't heard from Elvis since the morning of the dance, and I hadn't seen him at his favorite diner after school," he recalled. "It wasn't like Elvis to stay out of touch, and I was worried that something was very wrong. The Presleys didn't have a phone, so I stopped by unannounced on my way home."

Gladys was more annoyed than concerned about her son, assuming he was with Dixie. On his way home, Earl decided she was probably right. "Elvis and Dixie were probably parked in some lovers' lane, still swept away by the emotions from the prom. Everyone knew that was the one night of the year that many couples went all the way, as we called it then. Maybe Elvis just hadn't come up for air yet."

Earl didn't think about it again until Elvis showed up at Earl's house a few days later looking ragged and raw. His eyes were ringed with dark circles, he had lost weight, and his whole body seemed to shake—even his hair hung in limp strands over his ears and across his forehead.

This wasn't a young man in the throes of romance; this was a spurned lover grieving. Elvis announced Dixie had broken up with him. Or more accurately, she had dashed his dreams by turning down his marriage proposal, so he saw no reason in seeing her anymore.

The night had started out the way Elvis envisioned it would. When he picked Dixie up, she looked like a princess. He remembered shivering as he pinned on her corsage and swore she shivered, too. On the way to the dance, she smelled the flower and told Elvis she was going to put it in a scrapbook and keep it forever. To him, that was as good as a profession of true love.

At the prom they slow danced, and every time Elvis looked at Dixie, he thought his heart would burst. On the way to the restaurant, unable to contain his feelings, Elvis blurted out a proposal. Shocked but not wanting to hurt him, Dixie tried to explain that while she cared for him a great deal, she wasn't ready to settle down with anyone. They spent the rest of the night in an uncomfortable silence, and when he dropped her off, he knew she was saying goodbye for more than just the night.

Dixie was also upset at the way it ended, having assumed since Elvis wanted to pursue a singing career, they would sort of naturally go their separate ways after high school. When Earl called to see how she was doing, she confided in him: "I do love Elvis, I really do. I think he's one of the most special people I'll ever meet. He's fun to be around, we had a great time together, and I'll always be his friend, but . . . I'm just not *in* love with him. I can just tell the difference."

Heartbroken, disillusioned, humiliated, angry, and bereft, Elvis ultimately decided his mother had been right. "She always told me not to believe any thing a silly girl tells you. They lie all the time … Mama told me not to get all wrapped up. She said Dixie would end up hurting me 'cause she was only a silly girl. I shoulda listened."

The next time Earl went over to see Elvis, he recalled, "Elvis was sprawled on the couch, looking pathetic. Gladys sat next to him, stroking his head, smoothing back the strands of hair, looking satisfied, almost smug.

"As we were ready to walk out the door, Gladys grabbed Elvis and held him close. *'Just you remember, nobody loves you like I do. You always got me.'* Translated to mean—you best not put any girl before your mama again. Dixie's turndown was vindication and proof of that. Gladys wanted to be everything to Elvis and wanted more from him than what was right or healthy to expect.

Dixie had been Elvis's first love and the first girl who had shown him genuine affection and care in return. Like most humans when they lose that first great love, he honestly didn't believe he would ever find anyone else to fill the emptiness in his heart. He was sick with the fear of that loss.

Plus, Dixie had opened the door to his sexuality. He was still very attracted to her, felt possessive of her, and the thought of someone else having her was maddening—and demeaning. Suddenly all his old feelings of inadequacy flooded back, leaving him emotionally raw.

He had counted on Dixie to be his savior from a painful past and an unsure future. Her love had given him validity; without it, he felt he was sliding back down the mountain into the valley of worthlessness. His reactions were extreme; because he'd been such an extreme outcast throughout his life, his sense of loss was greater. His senses were deadened, and his body sagged inward.

Had Dixie said yes and married Elvis, arguably the very fabric of our culture and music would have been affected. It is quite probable Elvis would have settled down right away with a steady job and started a family. There are some who think he would have been a happier man in the long run.

Instead, her turndown set Elvis on a different path. He approached his adult life with an aching void inside him. Elvis eventually managed his anguish through anger and by developing an armor that no woman would ever penetrate to the depths Dixie had. He simply wasn't about to let any woman hurt him like that again. Unfortunately, it also ensured he'd never love that way again, either. Other than Gladys, Dixie was the last woman Elvis would treat with pure love and respect. His unreleased anger would flare up as mistreatment and callousness for the rest of his life.

Needless to say, the breakup with Dixie put a severe damper on Elvis's excitement and enthusiasm for graduation. He was visibly proud of his achievement, but it wasn't the special day he'd looked forward to—the start of his grown-up life with Dixie.

Even though he was depressed, he wasn't about to ignore graduation or disappoint his parents. They were so proud, they both cried on the last day of school. Neither Vernon nor Gladys had attended high school, so his accomplishment was incredibly important to them. A high school diploma for Elvis had been their one shared dream, and now it was fulfilled. In fact, he was one of the first on the Presley side to finish high school. He was eager to show up for commencement to hear his name called and have that diploma placed in his hand.

They celebrated by Gladys cooking dinner over at the Greenwoods' place, a special meal of pork chops, corn bread, black-eyed peas, and apple pie. Elvis chose not to attend any of the parties being thrown by classmates—the last thing he wanted was to run into Dixie somewhere. Instead, after dinner Elvis kept to himself and spent half the warm, still evening sitting in the corner of the back porch, strumming his guitar, occasionally humming.

Anyone looking through the Humes High 1953 yearbook would see a young man who seemed to have finally fit it. Next to his senior photo it said "Major: Shop, History, English" and "Activities: ROTC, News Club, History Club, Speech," the last three joined at Dixie's suggestion.

But open the front cover and only one person had signed it.

His diploma now in hand, Elvis wasn't sure what to do with himself, feeling directionless. So the week after graduation, Elvis went job hunting with a vengeance. He signed up at the local unemployment office, scoured the want ads, and went on a number of interviews.

He was willing to do almost anything, but he needed to make a decent wage because once again, he was the family's main breadwinner. Gladys had lost her job after staying home a full week, suffering from "exhaustion" that she claimed was caused by the strain of working full time in poor health during Elvis's senior year.

Seeing Gladys take to her bed and hearing her weak voice stabbed Elvis with guilt, and he took the first good-paying job offered—as a factory worker for Precision Tool Company. He hated it. The working conditions were cramped, the boss looked over his shoulder, and worst of all, he was forced to wear a scarf over his hair.

Elvis gave Gladys half of his check for bills and living expenses and kept the rest. This arrangement saved him from going through the exercise of having to ask his mother for money that was his to begin with. Despite Elvis having cash in his pocket, his mood was definitely subdued, as he dreaded having to go to work every day.

A few weeks later, the unemployment office left a message for Elvis with their neighbor that Crown Electric was looking for a driver who could fix his own truck if anything went wrong with it. Elvis jumped at the chance. The starting salary was $45 a week and he wouldn't be cooped up inside a steaming factory all day. Best of all, he wouldn't have to wear a scarf.

For as thrilled as he was with the new job, he was resentful that he was carrying the load by himself with no help from his father. But Vernon didn't mind living hand to mouth, and his sense of freedom was more important to him than the security of a weekly paycheck or his family's peace of mind. And now that Elvis was out of school and officially a man, Vernon was content to let him assume complete responsibility. That fact really burned Elvis, but he refused to confront Vernon, keeping his feelings inside when his father was around.

Even though Elvis was now working 40 hours a week, he had more free time on his hands than he'd ever known. After his shift was over, the rest of the day was his own. He had no more classes to study for, and Gladys had given up trying to get Elvis to stay home with her, especially since he had somewhere he'd really rather be. Beale Street drew him like a moth to a lantern, and during that summer of '53, Elvis became a regular at the assortment of clubs that dotted the area.

Although Elvis talked nonstop about singing, he didn't have a clue how to go about breaking in to show business. One day he'd be wildly confident, the next day he'd be depressed and sure he was wasting his time on an unattainable dream, but it was never out of his mind. Being around musicians fed both his dreams and his passion.

When he first started going to Beale Street, he'd mostly just wander around and stand out on the sidewalk, listening to the blues musicians playing inside, just like at that church back in Tupelo. After a while, he finally built up the courage to walk inside—and found heaven. Sultry music filtered through the smoky haze of the club and settled on Elvis like a flannel blanket. He slid onto a stool and let the atmosphere enfold him. People sat by themselves nursing drinks or enjoyed the company of friends in lively groups.

He quickly adopted Beale Street as his own, even though he was one of the few white people at the time to hang out there regularly. Being some kind of outcast was old news to Elvis, but here the music gave him a sense of belonging even if his skin color said otherwise.

Beale Street became his favorite shopping center as well. There was a famous clothing store there called Lansky Brothers, where many of the local black artists shopped. The store carried a dizzying array of styles and colors and patterns—just the sort of clothes Elvis dreamed about. The prices were way out of his range, but Elvis loved walking through the racks, browsing and daydreaming. He went in so often he got to know the owners, who told Elvis about secondhand stores where he could get similar styles he could afford. Elvis always remembered how nice the owners were to him, making time for him when they didn't have to. After he was famous, Elvis bought half of his wardrobe from Lansky's and would remember them every Christmas.

Gladys worried about Elvis spending the day driving after staying out late the night before, but he laughed off her concerns. He was not about to give up the one bright spot in his life. Since Memphis was home to a variety of nightlife, Elvis didn't restrict his evenings out to just blues clubs. Bluegrass and country bars also had their own strongholds, and Elvis cruised through them all, taking in the different styles and sounds. He watched the performers and visualized himself up on stage, playing to the noisy crowds, and geared himself up for that eventuality. But the clubs satisfied more than his thirst for music; they were the venues where Elvis unleashed his sexuality.

The country-western bars especially attracted a lot of women, who hung around looking for companionship or just a drink. Elvis quickly noticed that singers were never at a loss for female company after a set. As he spent more time at predominantly white bars, Elvis found himself the center of unfamiliar attention from women who saw through the loud clothes to his sexual potential. These bar groupies weren't simple and pure "good girls," and Elvis enthusiastically immersed himself in their open arms.

Normally, Elvis was uncomfortable talking about sex, but he couldn't contain himself after finally losing his virginity to an older woman named Laura. Needing to tell someone, he tracked Earl down at their favorite diner hangout, still wired.

"There ain't nothing better," he announced. "It makes you feel so . . . *strong*. I hardly slept but felt like I could go on forever. Now I know what women are best for," he laughed. "There's lots of girls to pick from, and I'm gonna do some plucking."

Laura was the first in a steady stream of one- or two-night stands. If the girl didn't have her own apartment, they would drive to a secluded spot and climb in the back seat of Elvis's car. As he got more experience, Elvis developed a sexiness that bubbled to the surface, attracting even more ladies to fulfill his desires.

Elvis used women with relish but considered them cheap. His attitude toward them was harsh, even hostile, once the sex was over. More than once after finishing with one girl, he'd go back to the bar and pick up another for more. The last thing Elvis wanted was to get emotionally involved, so the women he slept with were truly objects for sex, not human beings with feelings.

For someone who slept with a couple girls a week, Elvis was still shy around proper girls. Sex became a great equalizer for Elvis. He felt inferior around most girls, especially those with any kind of breeding—unless he'd conquered them in the bedroom, proving their cheapness and his superiority. As he got older, knocking good girls off their pedestals became a favorite pastime; every time he succeeded in doing it, his disillusion with women grew. All of them failed the Gladys comparison test.

The control and power that casual sex gave him over women was quite a contrast to his home life, where Gladys still ruled the roost through guilt and obligation. Unwilling to let her hold over him loosen any more than it already had, she waited up for Elvis every night, no matter how much he begged her not to. But with both Vernon and Elvis out most nights, leaving her alone, she tortured herself with alcohol-fueled visions of abandonment. Her biggest fear was that Elvis would find someone and want to move out on his own. She'd get so upset he'd have to promise to never leave her alone—his juggling act of trying to make his own life while being Gladys's emotional touchstone as difficult as ever.

DIFFICULT BEGINNINGS

Elvis's first public performance after high school was a disaster of such proportions he was convinced his career was over minutes after it began.

Hernando's Hideaway, one of the seedier clip joints Elvis frequented, would hire anyone brave—or stupid—enough to perform. Elvis offered to entertain three nights for free—music to the owner's ears. All the singers he had talked to told him the same thing: the only way to learn to be a performer was to just do it. Plus, record producers and deejays often showed up at amateur nights, and those were the people who could make or break a career.

He was apprehensive but determined to go through with it, although he could have barely picked a more difficult audience. Hernando's was filled with a hard-drinking, crew cut–sporting, macho crowd, and it turned out to be a miserable night all around. Outside it was pouring rain. Inside, Hernando's was cold, drafty, muddy, and reeked of mildew. Everything was damp to the touch, and the clientele seemed particularly edgy. Tables were carelessly scattered around a tiny platform that doubled as a stage, and there were as many bouncers as there were customers. Hernando's wasn't allowed to sell alcohol, but if customers brought their own bottles, they'd serve it in paper cups, so the liquor flowed freely and often.

The manager introduced Elvis, and Elvis stepped up on the tiny stage accompanied by only his guitar. When a few burly guys at the next table guffawed at his outfit—green pants, checkered jacket, pink shirt—it was clear that a long night loomed ahead.

Elvis sang a selection of current hits on the country charts, and his performance was a complete bust. His natural charisma deserted him, leaving him appearing awkward and unattractive, pale and damp with nervous sweat. His voice, normally so rich and resonant, sounded squeaky and unnatural. Instead of singing in his own distinctive style, he tried to copy a voice he'd heard on the radio and ended up sounding like a bad recording. To top it off, he strummed his guitar with no sense of rhythm and gave the overall impression of someone who didn't know what the hell he was doing.

Midway through the first song, a few people laughed. During the second song, some hecklers joined in. Beer-soaked men asked Elvis what he did with the money his parents had given him for singing lessons, and what beauty parlor did his hair. By the third song, Elvis's voice tightened up, choked by his humiliation. He stopped altogether after an empty bottle was thrown in his general direction, followed by a littering of wadded-up paper cups. He got off the stage and walked straight out the back door, shutting out the laughter behind him.

He sat in his car, unable to keep from crying, wishing the earth would just swallow him up. When he talked to Earl about it, embarrassment turned to self-pity. "It wasn't just the singing they didn't like, it was me. This was a stupid idea from the start and now I don't know what I'm gonna do."

But that night when he got home, Elvis couldn't bring himself to tell Gladys what had happened, so he lied and told her it had gone well. The pride in her face was so bright, he knew he had to try again. He tried to rebuild his confidence by remembering the applause from the fair and the talent show, but the next time he performed, he was tense like never before, expecting to see more beer bottles flying through the air at him.

He stood off to the side of the stage, taking deep breaths to calm himself. After his introduction, he got up on stage, fixed his eyes at the rear of the room, and started singing. The songs were the same, but this time he sang them in the style that came naturally to him, in a strong, melodious voice. Nobody paid much attention one way or another, and while there were not bottles or hecklers, there was no applause, either. Elvis was just background noise.

But when his set was done, he bounded off the stage flushed with a sense of accomplishment. It hadn't been a performance of the ages, but it had been good enough—enough to keep his dream alive. From that night on, he pursued singing with a newfound vigor. Coming so close to losing it had done the trick.

In the months that followed, Elvis searched out every amateur night or honky-tonk looking for free talent in the greater Memphis area. He never had a regular set, just whatever was popular on the radio at the moment. He might hear something on the radio while driving to a club, and although totally unprepared, he would try to sing it anyway. Even if he knew only half the words, he would give it a shot because it was a hit song.

Some nights were good, but many were bad. He never developed a thick skin and always took audience apathy or jeering personally. What he did was synonymous with who he was, so he construed any criticism of his singing as a personal rejection and it made him angry—and more determined. "I'll show 'em. One day they'll see," he'd say whenever an audience gave him a cool reception.

As the year came to a close, Elvis wrote down his plans for the future—his day, his week, his life. Topping his list was marriage and children, followed by caring for Gladys. Singing came in a surprising third. Sometimes, after a rough weekend of "clubbing," Elvis found his confidence sagging and his enthusiasm waning, and singing was in danger of being erased off the list altogether.

It was during a low period that Elvis decided he needed something to fall back on and announced he was studying to be an electrician. Since he couldn't afford to go to college, he decided to teach himself and checked a stack of books out of the library.

Elvis doggedly studied his books at night during the week, but for all his efforts, he wasn't learning anything. Still, he refused to give up. His fledgling music career was stalled in Memphis's lesser honky-tonks, and he felt pressure to secure a solid future of some kind in order to take care of his mother. "God, I wish Jesse was here," he'd often say. "We could take turns looking after Mama."

His parents were proud of his attempt to become an electrician, but Vernon was realistic about Elvis's abilities and forbid him from practicing at home. Surprisingly, though, Vernon was supportive of Elvis's singing aspirations, even though he didn't believe those dreams would ever be fulfilled. He assumed Elvis would eventually give up and settle down.

Gladys loved the idea of her son being a singer. But her biggest worry was that Elvis would fall into a bad crowd at the clubs and be led down an all-too-familiar Presley path. Everybody had concerns about Elvis. Vernon generally kept his private, but he worried that his wife's attachment to their son was not altogether healthy. He was also aware that neither would particularly miss him if he walked out one day and never returned. But Vernon suffered his hurts in silence.

In January 1954, Elvis went back to the Memphis Recording Studio, where he had previously paid $4 to make a record for Gladys's birthday. It had been such a hit with his mother, he thought he'd try the same tactic out on a girl he was desperate to impress and get into bed.

That he ever made that first record for Gladys was a fluke.

Elvis was on his way home after his last delivery of the day when he suddenly remembered it was her birthday. He knew she'd be waiting at home, anticipating his present. If he walked in empty-handed, she'd be bitterly disappointed.

As Elvis racked his brain trying to think of a gift that would make her happy, he drove by the Memphis Recording Service (MRS), and the answer jumped out at him: "Make Your Own Record—Only $4.00."

He had seen the sign countless times before without giving it much thought, but on this day—call it fate, happenstance, destiny, or whatever—Elvis pulled into the MRS parking lot and went in to make his mother a recording.

The secretary in charge of the public recordings had been so impressed with his unique sound that she took a copy of his first record to MRS owner Sam Phillips, who was also the founder of Sun Records. Phillips listened politely, then promptly forgot about it. But the secretary didn't.

So when Elvis returned, she remembered him immediately and greeted him warmly. After several minutes of blatant flirting, Elvis recorded "Casual Love" and "I'll Never Stand in Your Way," aware of both his rapt audience and the power he could exert with his voice. When he left, he had the secretary's phone number tucked safely away in his pocket.

That night at Leonard's Drive-in, Elvis presented the record to a petite blonde sitting in a corner booth with three of her girlfriends. The girl blushed under Elvis's steady gaze but didn't avert her eyes when she agreed to a date the following Saturday.

"Maybe I ought to have you autograph this now for when you get famous," she said, holding the record to her chest.

"You don' need my name on a piece of paper—you got me," he said, lightly squeezing her shoulder.

In less than a year, the whole country would have Elvis.

Chapter 7

HONING THE TALENT

Desperate to find new talent for his small-time label, Sam Phillips finally gave in and listened to the second recording by the kid with the sideburns his persistent secretary kept nagging him about. Phillips heard the sound of money buried under the harsh static of a cheap recording.

When the wind-up alarm clock rattled him awake, Elvis had no inkling this was the day that would forever divide his life into before and after. He staggered into the bathroom for his clothes and got ready for work in the darkened apartment, careful not to wake his parents. He dressed quickly but spent considerable time greasing and combing his hair. He left, shutting the door gently behind him, to face another day of driving and daydreaming.

The Presleys still had no phone, but their neighbor Jim gave Elvis free rein to use his. When Elvis got home from work that afternoon, he found a note on his apartment door to call Sun Studios as soon as possible. Elvis assumed it must be the cute little secretary being forward and went to return the call with bedroom thoughts dancing in his head. When a man claiming to be Mr. Phillips answered, Elvis immediately thought it was a practical joke, but disbelief turned to excitement, then terror, then back to elation in quick turns as Phillips warmly complimented his voice on the four songs he had recorded. Phillips then explained he needed a demo singer for a ballad called "Without You" and asked if Elvis would be interested.

Gladys came running out of the apartment at the sound of Elvis's screaming and was relieved to see by his flushed, smiling face that he was excited, not being murdered. While other startled neighbors peeked out from behind their doors, Elvis grabbed Gladys in the dreary hallway and spun her around in a would-be waltz before lifting her off the ground in a bear hug.

She squealed girlishly. "Elvis Aron, you put me down. What's got into you? What'll the neighbors think?"

"Let them think what they want, Mama. I did it, I finally did it."

Elvis stuttered out what had happened, and Gladys cried tears of happiness, even though she had no idea what a demo was until he explained it to her. Elvis was beside himself, wondering what it all meant—if anything at all. He was unable to sit or stand in any one place. His emotions needed more space than their tiny apartment could give, so he spent the evening driving the streets of Memphis, too preoccupied to stop at any of his usual haunts. As the night wore on, nervousness and self-doubt gradually elbowed aside the heady thrill he had first experienced, and his mind raced into dark and frightening corners. By the time he got home, Elvis felt sick with anxiety. Drained and tired but unable to sleep, Elvis lay on the couch wide awake, staring at the darkness as he tried to see the future.

The rest of the week passed in tantalizing slow motion. Elvis practiced singing until he was nearly hoarse. Elvis showed up at Leonard's a few days after his big day in the studio. Instead of being full of stories, he was subdued and reluctant to talk about what happened until pressed.

"I don't know why but it was just awful. I was just awful," he told Earl Greenwood. "It was a pretty enough song but I couldn't get ahold of it. Mr. Phillips made me sing it over and over, with a band, without a band … He tried being nice but he hated the way I sang it, everyone could tell. Nobody would look me in the eye. It was so humiliating. I wanted to run outa there and not look back."

Then he looked up with a disbelieving, trembling sigh. "I couldn't believe it when he told me to come back the next afternoon 'cause he wanted me to try something else. I'd a never let me back in the door."

When Elvis returned the following day, Phillips introduced him to two musicians: Scotty Moore and Bill Black. Sam realized Elvis's biggest problem was a lack of training and experience, so he arranged for Elvis to practice his singing using Scotty and Bill as a back-up combo—who for their part thought it was a big waste of time.

Elvis spent hours at Scotty's house, rehearsing a number of ballads Sam had given him. With his musicians backing him up, Elvis tried out his new material at a couple of clubs with typically mixed and muted reactions. Not surprisingly, when they went back to the studio to try another demo, the results were disappointingly familiar.

Elvis knew he was on the brink of disaster and was paralyzed at the thought of blowing this opportunity. He kept telling himself to just relax, but his constricted throat betrayed him. With each take, the tension in the studio thickened, straining everyone's nerves. A tight-jawed Phillips called for five, and Elvis was left ominously alone. During the break, Elvis tried to calm his escalating panic by singing—except this time instead of a schmaltzy ballad, Elvis stood up and shook to the beat of an upbeat blues tune, "That's All Right, Mama." The sounds of his lilting high octaves brought them all running.

"They had me singing songs I just wasn't comfortable with, that's all," he later realized. "When I stood up and sang a song I liked, that made all the difference. I need something I can move to."

Sam knew a winner when he heard one and was smart enough to go with it. He recorded "That's All Right, Mama," and Elvis cut a snappy "Blue Moon of Kentucky" for the flip side.

Elvis showed up at Leonard's soon after in a state resembling shock and disbelief. "None of it seems real. The day started out so bad then everything happened at once," including Phillips's promise to get Elvis's song played on the radio.

Earl was more excited about this sudden turn of events than Elvis, who was still tentative and didn't want to tell anyone else, especially his mother, the news. "I can't believe it'll really happen, y'know? I don't wanna get all excited over nothing—every time I do, it gets ruined. I don't wanna jinx it."

That said, he couldn't help but let his imagination roam. "I wish I knew what it all meant—it just don't seem real to me. I ain't never been lucky like this. Good things never happen to us."

A disc jockey named Dewey Phillips (no relation to Sam) agreed to play Elvis's version of "That's All Right, Mama" on his station, WHBQ, as a favor to the label owner. Elvis knew exactly when his record was going to be played, but he refused to listen. He was too scared he'd see disappointment in Gladys's eyes or be ridiculed by others if it sounded awful. So he turned the station on for his parents, then he left to go on a long car ride by himself, feeling sick to his stomach from nerves.

Vernon and Gladys were waiting for him when he got home and were genuinely thrilled, but he took their review as biased. What finally convinced him he hadn't been a disaster was when acquaintances came up to congratulate him, and girls found excuses to talk to him. Once again, he basked in the acceptance and read it as love.

The effect on Elvis was visible. His chest puffed out with pride, he laughed and smiled more with strangers, he flirted more openly with girls, and he even stuttered less. He was trying on popularity and liked the way it fit. Within a week, Sun received over 5,000 orders from people who wanted a copy of the record, and Elvis was a local hit—and destined to stay one. Despite an aggressive mailing by Phillips to deejays in all the major markets, Elvis's record never heard the light of day. It was a "country song" from a "country label," and Top 40 stations weren't interested.

When he was finally comfortable enough to listen to himself on the radio, he was both pleased and critical. "Every time it comes on, all I hear are the mistakes I made. If it wasn't for the guys in back of me playing, they'd be throwing bottles at the radio," he laughed. But his desire for perfection couldn't diminish the pride he felt, or hide his disbelief. "I just can't get over it. It was too easy. I thought you were supposed to have to work hard for a singing career."

As word spread among his acquaintances, Elvis became a minor celebrity at the diners and bars where he spent his time. People who had barely given him the time of day before were suddenly going out of their way to say hello or buy him a drink. Elvis especially loved the increased female attention.

That initial rush of overt self-importance went over better in the bars than it did at home. Gladys was floating with joy over Elvis's leap from obscurity, but she was upset at how infrequently he was home. The first time Elvis dismissed Gladys in a sassy tone, she reminded him in no uncertain terms that she was still his mother and was to be treated accordingly. He was leaving to go bar hopping when Gladys asked what time he'd be home—a ritual they went through every night.

"When I feel like it, that's when," he answered, not hiding his irritation. Gladys was up and on him in a flash, grabbing his arm in a painful grip. "I don' care how many records you got playing, you better learn respect. I ain't one of your bar whores and don't like being treated like one. You talk to me in that tone again, I'll slap that attitude outta you and don't think I won't. I was afraid you'd pick up bad habits hanging out in bars filled with loose women and loafers. Don't make me sorry you're my boy."

Her words stung worse than any slap could, and Elvis apologized, chastened and deflated. Having the night off from performing, Elvis cruised the bars that had become his home away from home, intent on finding a woman. He needed to regain the potency his mother had sucked out of him. It didn't take him long to find a willing partner, and just like other similar encounters, he left feeling superior but empty.

LEARNING THE ROPES

Sam Phillips's strategy to establish Elvis was to book him into any decent club and bar in the greater Memphis area, which were many. Phillips believed in Elvis's talent but worried at his lack of professionalism—he was often late and usually unprepared to sing, having failed to familiarize himself with the music. Sam realized part of the problem was his young singer's lack of musical training and knowledge. He insisted on regular rehearsals with the combo, so Elvis would go straight from his shift at Crown to either the Sun studios or the club where they were performing. Before long, he was about to drop from the grueling schedule. Something had to give, but the prospect of making a commitment either way terrified Elvis.

Even though he was paid a modest fee for performing, and was assured by Phillips that he was on his way to a solid singing career, Elvis clung to the job at Crown—part of him convinced his moment of glory would blow away any day. Driving the truck was a sure thing. If he gave it up, there'd be no more waiting for the future to happen. It would be time to succeed or fail and find once and for all if he had what it took. Elvis finally took the decisive step the day Phillips gave him his first royalty check for $200. That kind of money-making potential was all the incentive he needed to stop playing it safe.

The first thing Elvis bought was a dress and a nice pair of shoes for Gladys—probably the nicest shoes she'd ever owned. She kept them in a plastic bag beside her bed and looked at them every time she walked by the door. More than anything, those shoes symbolized where the family had come from and where Elvis hoped to take them. Vernon thought it was a waste of money to buy shoes Gladys wouldn't wear (her feet were too swollen), but Elvis dismissed those concerns with a shrug, too pleased with himself over giving Gladys something Vernon had never been able to. Gladys just enjoyed having nice things to show off. Elvis also paid to have a phone installed, prompting Vernon to dryly observe, "Too bad we ain't got anyplace to go or friends to call."

Despite her excitement over Elvis's success, Gladys fretted over his failure to attend church regularly. Elvis downplayed it, promising he would start going again once his schedule calmed down. But she was afraid that Elvis was playing with his soul by turning his back on church. Regardless of what Elvis said, Gladys knew avoiding church was the same thing as avoiding God. Without that guidance, she worried Elvis would stumble down a reckless path and not find his way back. For all the insecurities that hounded him, she could see that Elvis feared the wrong things. She had lived long enough to know that people are their own worst enemies. The only way she knew to protect him was to be there to watch out for him, but she felt him slipping away.

Cruising the streets, Elvis sang and whistled, smiling at every girl he passed. He had good reason to be in such a lighthearted mood. In July 1954, "That's All Right, Mama" was number three on the local country-and-western sales charts and went on to become number one in the Memphis area, despite the reluctance of many deejays to play the record on white stations. Because it sounded like the blues, or what was considered "Negro music," they assumed Elvis was black, so his exposure was confined to the Memphis area.

Despite his arguments to the contrary, Elvis Presley was a budding country star. On the strength of the record's popularity in Memphis, Phillips managed to get an audition for Elvis at the Grand Ole Opry, assuring him it was just a formality and he was a shoo-in to be invited to perform. Even though he wasn't keen on country, Elvis knew how important an appearance on the Opry could be for his career, and his head was already swimming with visions of immediate, national stardom. In his mind, this was it.

Elvis asked Earl to accompany him to Nashville. They drove in one car and his musicians, Bill Black and Scotty Moore, and their equipment followed in another, and the abbreviated caravan sped with positive purpose toward the shrine of country music. During the drive, Elvis was relaxed and supremely confident, almost cocky. He shouted out the window as they neared Nashville. He was all wound up, and the words and pent-up frustrations spilled out.

"No more driving a truck, no more projects, no more being spit on by people thinking they're better. I told you all along I'd show 'em, didn' I? Wait'll those stuffed shirts at the Opry sees us—we're gonna turn them on their ears."

When they pulled into the parking lot behind the Opry, it wasn't the grand spectacle Elvis had been expecting. "I seen barns that look better," he joked, slightly disappointed.

They found the stage manager, who stared at Elvis as if he were a new species, and were told the time of the audition and pointed toward the backstage area where they were to wait. While the musicians carried in their instruments, Elvis carried his wardrobe, an eye-shocking Beale Street special he planned to wear on the show that night.

He practiced with his band a short time and exchanged a few pleasantries with a couple of other performers waiting their turn, mostly a friendly group named the Jordanaires. Elvis made jokes and exuded a relaxed assurance, but his constant movement and an unconscious tugging at his sideburns hinted at his nervousness as the time for the audition neared.

When the stage manager called his name, he told Elvis he had just five minutes. Elvis and his band moved onto the great stage, and he looked out at the biggest auditorium he'd ever seen. It truly was a grand building, and the decades of tradition it housed made Elvis feel suddenly small and insignificant, which in turn made him angry and determined to prove his worth. The stage manager impatiently paced near the wings and his irritated sighs made Elvis flinch. The Opry official auditioning him, Mr. Denny, sat waiting with an unreadable expression on his face.

Elvis took a deep breath, gave his musicians a quick nod, and turned to face his impassive audience. He sang "That's All Right, Mama" and "Blue Moon of Kentucky" the way nobody there had ever heard. In the confines of the building that *is* country-western music, it was plain as day to see that Elvis was cut from a different cloth. With his unique riffs, and hips and knees swaying to the music, Elvis unwittingly proved his own point—he was no more classic country than Hank Williams was a jazz singer. The songs might have been country standards, but to the judge's finely tuned ears, they no doubt seemed blasphemy.

When he was finished, there was an almost eerie silence from Mr. Denny. "Thank you very much, Mr. Presley. I'm sorry, but I don't think your act is quite right for the Opry at this time."

Elvis just stood there, unwilling to give up. "I know we started a little slow, can't we try something else?"

"That's not needed. We appreciate your visit, but maybe you ought to go back to driving that truck, son."

Elvis was stunned and turned to his musicians, who avoided his eyes. They packed up quickly and quietly with undue concentration. The next set of performers coming on stage gave Elvis a wide berth as he walked off, hanging his head in shame. The burly stage manager laughed derisively as he passed. "Boy, you get a reg-u-lar haircut and take some singing lessons, and maybe you'll be good enough for the Opry, but I surely doubt it."

Elvis's face fell, and he visibly deflated under the verbal punch. The earlier swagger and cockiness were replaced by teary-eyed insecurity. Elvis couldn't meet the stage manager's mocking eyes and hurried off the stage and ran straight for his car. The musicians leaned in the door and made a sincere effort to cheer him up.

"The Opry's run by a stuffy old bunch; everyone knows they like to make you kiss ass a bit before letting you on their show. Don't worry about it. You'll make it next time," Scotty said. "They don't like anybody who don't have a Nashville address, neither," Bill added.

Elvis nodded but didn't respond before he screeched away, the accelerator accurately gauging his humiliation. Most performers equate appreciation of their art with an acceptance of themselves as people, but it was magnified and exaggerated with Elvis. Embarrassment became humiliation, disappointment became despair. Every hurt and setback became catastrophic failure and a reason to quit.

"I don' know how I coulda let myself be so stupid, thinking I was gonna make something special of myself. Any time in my life I expected something good to happen, it just blows up in my face."

Elvis was inconsolable and so upset that he refused to go back and retrieve the unworn outfit he'd left behind in the Opry waiting room.

It was a long, uncomfortable drive home. Elvis's granite jaw finally loosened as he drove into Memphis, and tears suddenly flooded his cheeks. "What am I gonna tell Mama? How am I gonna tell her I ain't good enough? She's gonna be so disappointed in me. And everybody I told are all gonna be laughing at me behind my back. I'll never be able to face them anymore."

Elvis parked his car a block away from home, in front of a deserted, condemned building. He got out, slamming the door behind him, and walked into the debris-strewn area. He picked up a large board and suddenly began smashing it violently into the ground, cursing and crying. He swung the board wildly until it was reduced to splinters, then sank to his knees, choking on the dust and the taste of despair.

Although Elvis had convinced himself he would immediately be dropped from the label, Sam Phillips shrugged off Elvis's abysmal showing at the Opry and spent considerable time assuring Elvis he didn't need the Opry. Elvis was convinced his dream was dead but agreed to keep going for the time being, having nothing better to do. In addition to the regular rounds of clubs, Phillips arranged for Elvis to appear for a week at the Louisiana Hayride, the same place he'd won $50 in an amateur contest just a few months earlier.

Elvis was excited at both the gig and going on the road. He'd never spent a week away from home before and was anticipating the anonymous freedom of being away from familiar places and faces, of not having Gladys looking over his shoulder. Gladys, needless to say, was far from thrilled, but Elvis paid little attention to her fretting and was relieved when Vernon hushed her so he wouldn't have to.

On the drive to Louisiana, Elvis felt oddly removed from all he'd been through, as if it were really happening to someone else. It was hard for Elvis to comprehend all that had happened to him in the span of a few months. He'd gone from driving a truck to being on the radio, moved out of brawl-prone dives to more respectable clubs, had a record label behind him, and was known to thousands of people. He wanted to feel different inside and tried to adopt an appropriate outer attitude. But inside, he felt as insecure as ever—certain he was going to fall flat on his face at any given moment and lose it all. He wasn't so much going forward as running scared at falling back. No Presley had ever been able to hang on to anything for very long, and that legacy filled him with unease.

Colonel Parker steered Elvis away from country music and encouraged Elvis to seduce audiences with his natural sex appeal. Even though he wasn't a skilled guitarist, in his early days as a performer, Elvis would keep the guitar with him on stage as a kind of security blanket (1950s). Courtesy of Photofest.

Early in his career, Elvis enjoyed the crowds huddled outside his home and would frequently invite female fans into Graceland (1950s). But over time, the pressure of always being in the public eye and knowing his every move was watched prompted Elvis to stay sequestered inside his home during the day and only venture out late at night. Courtesy of Photofest.

Although Elvis was often intimidated by his Hollywood leading ladies, he was also invariably attracted to them—none more so than his Viva Las Vegas costar Ann-Margret (1964). They began a torrid affair that left Elvis torn between the red-haired beauty and Priscilla. But in the end, Elvis ended his relationship with Ann-Margret and a short time later finally married Priscilla. Courtesy of Photofest.

Although pictures presented them as fairy-tale newlyweds, what the public didn't know was that Elvis had felt pressured into marrying Priscilla (1967). Although she hoped that being married would improve their relationship, in many ways it was the beginning of the end. After their daughter, Lisa Marie, was born nine months later, Elvis was never physically intimate with his wife again. Courtesy of Photofest.

His controversial control over Elvis's finances and career earned Colonel Parker the reputation of being a Svengali-type manager; there is little argument that his shrewd business sense was instrumental in Elvis's rise to fame. Parker encouraged Elvis to make films, such as Change of Habit (1969) instead of touring. Courtesy of Photofest.

In one of the more unusual photo-ops, Richard Nixon and Elvis pose for a picture after the former President presented Elvis with a special DEA badge, in appreciation for Elvis's stance on the war on drugs (1970). According to some of Elvis's entourage present at the event, Elvis was under the influence of pills when he visited the White House. Courtesy of Photofest.

Elvis's increasing dependence on drugs to control his anxiety and help him sleep began to take a visible toll by the 1970s. His once lean body turned bloated, his eyes were frequently glassy, his behavior became increasing erratic, and his overall health deteriorated, resulting in numerous hospital stays. Although his still performed to sold-out crowds in Las Vegas, he started seeing himself as a has-been. Courtesy of Photofest.

Chapter 8

PAINFUL LESSONS

Life on the road wasn't as exciting as Elvis expected. He still had trouble making friends with guys, although he had no trouble talking to the women he met in the bars. For the first time, he was able to spend the night with a woman and discover the joys of morning intimacy. The one-night stands he experienced in Louisiana didn't ease the loneliness he felt inside, but they helped fulfill his needs.

In addition to performing, Elvis also did a few radio commercials. His halting and mushy speech drove the technicians crazy, but he was so thrilled at being on the radio like a real celebrity he didn't notice their irritation. He was justifiably proud, even if the broadcast was local. The only notoriety any Presley had prior to Elvis was of the negative variety.

Elvis called Gladys every day, after his date from the previous night left, which often wasn't until the afternoon. She was overwhelmed at her baby doing radio commercials—she had never dared to even dream of such an honor but was still having a hard time understanding what it meant or where it would lead. Elvis didn't know either, but he dared to let himself begin to dream again.

As Elvis became established in the Memphis club scene, Sam Phillips suggested he consider hiring a manager. Managers at that time usually did little more than arrange bookings and handle whatever promotional work there might be. Elvis hated talking business because he felt ignorant and incapable. He avoided putting himself in a position of ridicule and preferred to let others deal with contracts, figures, and money matters. Up to now, he had let Sam Phillips handle any business arrangements, but

Phillips wasn't a manager. He had a record company to run and couldn't devote himself to Elvis.

More than anyone, it was Vernon who pushed Elvis to find additional business representation, urging him to find someone soon. An attorney might have made the most sense, but Southerners have tremendous distrust of lawyers, convinced they are out to use the law to cheat people.

Phillips suggested Elvis and his parents meet with Bob Neal, a Memphis deejay who worked at WMPS. Neal was personable and unthreatening, a good old boy who came across like a friendly uncle. Vernon was unimpressed, but Elvis felt comfortable with Neal's easygoing ways, and Gladys was charmed by his gentle manners. In the autumn of 1954, Elvis turned himself over to Neal, even though Neal had no prior managing experience. Because Elvis was underage, Vernon and Gladys signed the agreement on his behalf, although neither side opted to have a lawyer present—a move Neal would come to regret.

The first thing on Neal's list of things to do was to improve Elvis's image. He believed it was important to project a professional image and to live the part. He took Elvis to a car dealership and traded in his beat-up Cadillac for a brand-new Chevy, bought on credit. Elvis practically lived in the car for the first week—and certainly used it as a bedroom several times, ever mindful to make sure the seats were covered with towels.

Neal had no problem with Elvis's choice of clothes offstage, but he thought the loud colors and wild patterns distracted from his performance onstage, and he suggested solids. White was too Pat Boone-ish for Elvis, but black suited him and enhanced his dark looks. Wearing all black added an air of brooding mystery that pleased him. "They're my Outlaw of Love clothes," he laughed. "Women fall for the funniest things."

Elvis believed people were always staring at his "ugly hands" when he was singing, and so with Neal's approval, he gave in to vanity and had unsightly warts burned off his hands. Vernon thought it was a disgusting waste of money, but Neal defended Elvis, explaining that a performer needs to feel confident if he's going to perform at his best. After having the warts removed, he joked, "Now, if they could do something about my face."

In addition to playing Memphis clubs, Elvis performed at fairs, store openings, school proms, outdoor concerts, and bars from Tennessee to Kentucky to Mississippi to Louisiana and back. Elvis enjoyed playing up his limited celebrity to the wide-eyed country girls he met at rural bookings.

He was especially attracted to 15- and 16-year-olds, but he wasn't interested in finding himself a good, simple, and pure steady girlfriend. His obvious vulnerability attracted women, but he resisted letting anyone in, sticking to one-night stands.

Being the center of attention fed Elvis's fragile ego but caused its share of problems as well. More than once, his flirting got him into hot water and put him on dangerous ground. At one outdoor concert put on in conjunction with the opening of a new movie theater, Elvis flirted blatantly with a buxom blonde. He had never forgotten the advice he'd gotten way back at the Mississippi-Alabama State Fair: pick out someone and sing to them and pretend there's no one else in the room.

Later on at a nearby bar, Elvis and his musicians were relaxing with a beer when a tense, hard-bodied farmer walked up to Elvis and grabbed his collar. His breath smelled of homegrown liquor as he leaned down.

"You got no right messing with my girlfriend like that. She ain't stopped talking about the way you sang to her since this afternoon. I can't for the life of me figure out what she sees in some funny-looking, skinny runt like you. Must of been too much sun."

As soon as he walked out the door, Elvis let out a relieved sigh, and his drinking buddies broke into shouts of teasing laughter.

"That was a close one," Elvis admitted, smoothing out his crumpled shirt.

"Bob would've turned pasty if we'd brought you back stitched up like a quilt," said one of the musicians.

"Forget Bob—it's my mama you gotta worry about."

Other encounters weren't so easy. One afternoon at a country bar in Mississippi, Elvis cozied up to a woman who brazenly brushed his thigh with her fingertips under the table. He was ready to leave with her, but she teased him by wanting to finish her drink before leaving. Like a lot of women he met, she was attracted to the performer, with little interest in the man. Even if he was using them in a similar way, Elvis resented it—but not enough to walk away. He'd get even later when they were alone.

She finally finished her drink, and as they got up to leave, an irate man grabbed her from behind and spun her around. When Elvis reached out for her, the man reared back and took a swing at Elvis.

"Keep your filthy hands off my wife."

Elvis ducked and the punch grazed the side of his head. The man plowed into Elvis and they went flying over tables, arms flying about wildly, trying to land a blow. A crowd formed, urging them on and drowning out the pleading screams of the owner to stop. A bouncer finally separated them and pulled Elvis to a far corner. His hair was disheveled, he had a bloody nose and was winded, but other than that, he was fine.

The bouncer poked him in the chest and warned Elvis to stay away from other men's wives, then demanded, "Now who's gonna pay for the broken tables?"

"He started it, let him pay for it."

The bouncer shook his head. "I guess we'll let the sheriff figure it out. 'Course, fighting's against the law. I wouldn't be surprised if he threw the both of you in jail."

Elvis was familiar with country justice and knew he was beat. He reached in his pocket but had only a few dollars. "I'll pay, if I can call someone. I don't want no hard feelings. I really didn't know she was married."

After his performance that night, Elvis insisted they leave for home right away. He was not interested in staying one more night in the area, half afraid the husband would come gunning for him. He was finding out the hard way that fame and notoriety had some down sides, and one had to be careful of angry boyfriends, jealous husbands, and plucky rednecks who'd love to prove you weren't anything special and bring you down a notch. Even among acquaintances back home, he sensed that very few people seemed genuinely happy for him. Instead, they seemed poised for him to fail. It was hard for Elvis to completely enjoy any measure of success when he was always looking over his shoulder.

The only people he trusted, other than his family, were his audiences. When they clapped and whistled in appreciation of his music, of him, he found incentive in their acceptance and love.

By January 1955, his second record, "Good Rockin' Tonight," with "I Don't Care if the Sun Don't Shine" on the flip side, was released to only modest success. The cool reception to his follow-up single chipped away at Elvis's confidence and chilled his heart. He sank into a mild depression, worried he was stuck in quicksand.

"Bob keeps saying it takes a long time to make a name for yourself," he complained in an exasperated voice, "but this is taking forever and I don' have that kinda time. If I can only make enough money to get us our own home, that's all I want."

Personal appearances were still hit or miss. Elvis and his group, which now included drummer D. J. Fontana, were mostly a curiosity to the club patrons who preferred bluegrass to the blues. Sometimes the curiosity wore off quickly. At the Lakecliff Club, the house had been packed when they started their set, but by the end, they were playing to a nearly deserted room. The owner was so upset, he told them to skip their second set and clear out before they put him out of business for good.

A newspaper interview arranged by Neal with the *Memphis Press Scimitar* turned into another painful lesson of the price paid for being in the public eye. Had he been savvier, he would have coached Elvis, but Neal was too trusting and unknowledgeable, and the results were disastrous.

Elvis was nervous and eager to please the reporter assigned to write the story, and he answered each question as honestly as he could. He was especially open about Gladys. She was the number-one girl in his life, and he was dedicating his career to her. He thought she'd be delighted to see her name in the paper.

The published article was a small, uncomplimentary piece that had a mocking undercurrent. Earl Greenwood recalls that in the space of a few paragraphs, the writer called Elvis "a hillbilly cat," "the Tennessee Tornado," "the Memphis Flash," and "Mrs. Presley's son." He poked fun at Elvis's closeness to Gladys, implying he was a mama's boy, and insinuated Elvis was talented but simple.

The article shocked and stung Elvis, and he took out his hurt on Neal. Elvis lost confidence in Neal after that, especially since his career had once again stalled. Despite his sincere intentions and belief in Elvis's talent, Neal was hampered by his lack of experience and limited time, as he was still a working deejay. Neal sensed Elvis's frustration and felt under intense pressure to do something dramatic, to set ambitious new wheels in motion.

In March 1955, Neal took Elvis to New York to audition for Arthur Godfrey's *Talent Scouts* show, thinking it was a good way to get Elvis some much-desired national exposure. Neal took vacation time to drive up north with Elvis, who hated New York on sight—too many people moving too fast, paying too little attention to whether they knocked you over.

The production assistants running the rehearsals were brusque and rude, and they talked too quickly. Elvis got flustered and gave a subpar, awkward performance. Once again he was turned down, and once again he was discouraged—but not bitter. He had no use for New Yorkers, and their approval didn't matter to him then or later.

"New Yorkers're worse than the Opry," Elvis decided. "They barely let me finish. You'd of thought they were late for dinner. Can't imagine why anyone'd wanna waste their time in a place like that."

Still, Elvis was tired of playing the same clubs and was worried that Sam Phillips would lose interest. He was eager to find new momentum but protected himself from disappointment by downplaying the importance of a singing career.

"Sometimes I wish I was back at Crown," he'd announced. "If it weren't for Mama, I'd stop now, but I can't. I once said something to Mama about it, and she looked so upset and worried—I can't disappoint her like that. She'd think I was a quitter. I couldn't live with that."

Elvis continued playing clubs, parks, fairs, and anything else Neal could find, and he made a decent, if exhausting, living. As more people accepted his style, Elvis developed a small following and began to recognize some of his more ardent fans, although he paid little attention to the men in his audience. If he had, he might have noticed the heavyset man who had taken a particular interest in his career.

Colonel Tom Parker had followed Elvis for months, but hardly considered himself a fan. He took care to stay in the clubs' dark shadows, not wanting to tip his hand too soon. Parker had made a modest name for himself managing Eddy Arnold, but he was eager to make a star and create a lasting place for himself in music history. He was a man who craved wealth and the trappings of success.

He was also a man who wasn't all he seemed. For starters, he wasn't a colonel, he wasn't born in Huntington, West Virginia, his real name was not Tom Parker, and he wasn't even American. He was a clever, ambitious man who guarded his secrets closely while evading the Immigration Service and fulfilling his dream of being rich and famous—two goals seemingly at odds.

Parker was born in Breda, Netherlands, on June 26, 1909, and to America illegally when he was 18, entering the country in Tampa, Florida. Although few details are known about his early years in the United States, what is not debatable is that he never applied for a green card—although he apparently managed to join the U.S. Army. Once he got out of the service, he worked as a carny for Royal Amusement Shows; later he worked as a dogcatcher and ran a pet cemetery in Tampa during the 1940s.

Somehow, Parker made the jump to music and became a promoter, working with country stars Eddy Arnold, Minnie Pearl, and Hank Snow. It was through his friendship with Jimmy Davis, a popular singer-turned-governor of Louisiana, that Parker received the honorary rank of colonel as thanks for working on Davis's campaign.

His time with Eddy Arnold and the measure of success they shared merely whetted his appetite for more. In Elvis, he saw a virtual feast—a man who projected an ambiguous sexuality that, if properly handled, could draw both men and women. He viewed Elvis as a commodity to market and had put together a plan to do just that. Parker saw vividly what both Sam Phillips and Bob Neal had missed, and he knew that he could catapult Elvis the way neither of them ever could.

Parker was also smart enough to know how close-knit the Southern families were and was well aware of Elvis's special attachment to Gladys—he'd done his homework. With Elvis's parents on his side, Parker knew that Elvis would be a snap to win over.

Parker introduced himself to Vernon and Gladys at an upscale club. Gladys still refused to go to a bar, calling it distasteful for proper ladies, but clubs were another matter. She enjoyed the ladylike, colorful drinks and never got tired of watching Elvis sing. Vernon could take or leave the music, but he enjoyed the company of lively people—not to mention the lovely ladies.

Parker came on very low-key, not wanting to scare them off with a hard sell. Vernon immediately took to the Colonel because they spoke the same language—money—and were both schemers. Where Parker plotted for wealth and success, Vernon devoted his energy to avoiding work—different goals, similar personalities.

However, when Parker shook Gladys's hand, her skin crawled at his touch. She distrusted his beady, cold eyes and didn't believe his warm words about Elvis. With a mother's protectiveness, she instinctively suspected Parker was a man who cared only for himself, and she was irritated at Vernon for being so friendly.

Parker waited until Vernon asked before revealing his profession. Vernon wasted no time in seeking out Parker's advice, and the Colonel skillfully steered Vernon into his back pocket.

"That boy of yours is just a few months away from being a big star—it must be very exciting."

"It was at first. Things are supposed to be moving, but who knows. We'll prob'ly be sitting here five years from now."

"Not if you're willing to think big. If you keep thinking small, you'll stay small."

Vernon took the bait and began bad-mouthing Bob Neal.

Parker took the high road. "Vernon, Bob's doing all he can. He's worked hard for Elvis." Then the Colonel casually mentioned he was in Memphis scouting new talent and setting up interviews with prospective clients. He hesitantly admitted he was so impressed with Elvis, he had already arranged to meet with Bob Neal and Sam Phillips to offer his services as a consultant. By the time Vernon introduced Elvis to Parker when he joined their table, Vernon was sold. Parker said hello briefly, then excused himself, saying he had another act to catch across town. He left knowing Vernon would quickly go to work on his behalf.

But Elvis had no idea who Parker was. "Daddy, I let Bob handle business and just show up where and when he tells me. That's why I'm paying him fifteen percent."

"Ain't no way to run a career, boy. But maybe for once, Bob did something right. Mr. Parker knows what he's doing. Bob might learn a thing or two."

Elvis didn't admit it, but he wasn't too happy with Neal, either. At this point, he was frustrated enough to consider almost anything, even paying for a consultant (although he wasn't sure what one was and didn't expect much to come from it). People were always promising things but seldom came through.

Parker came aboard as an adviser and was a pleasant surprise. He backed up his professed interest in Elvis with time and suggestions, many of which grated Neal to no end. On the Colonel's strong recommendation, Elvis severed his association with the Louisiana Hayride, Neal's biggest coup, because the weekly drive was too time-consuming for a paycheck that Parker deemed way too small.

Neal was infuriated and turned to Elvis for support, but Elvis refused to get involved, partly because he figured he was paying them to handle business and partly because he was secretly relieved. Elvis was tired of packing his car up for the same trip every weekend, but more than that, there was the little matter of an affair with a certain young lady who had gotten more serious than Elvis ever intended.

She wasn't like the other girls he'd met who cruised the bars or hung around after performances. In fact, he wouldn't have met her at all if he hadn't driven by as she was on her way home. He recognized her from the audience and pulled over. They talked at the side of the road, Elvis attracted to her natural prettiness. She good-naturedly rebuffed his flirting but finally let him take her out for a burger. Although the evening ended with passionate kissing and touching, she refused to sleep with him that first weekend, but her smile held a seductive promise.

When they met up the following week, she wanted him as much as he wanted her. Except for his performance and his phone call to Gladys, they spent all day in bed, making love and talking. Elvis was touched by her honesty and loneliness. She was older than him by a year and very unhappy at home, where she was stuck taking care of her younger brothers and sisters most of the time while her parents played cards with drinking buddies. To get time for herself, she'd lie and say she was visiting friends in a nearby town, although she usually took a bus to Memphis by herself and saw a movie or just window shopped. She thought most of the guys in her town crude bores and hadn't found anyone she'd want to wake up with every morning.

Elvis had never met anyone like her, so sweet but so passionate. He felt a kinship with her and even let himself feel warmth, but the very fact that she desired Elvis enough to sleep with him was a strike against her in the "good, simple, and pure" department. Also holding him back from becoming emotionally involved was his driving ambition—he didn't want any entanglements because he was convinced they would hinder his budding career. He assumed she knew he was just passing through and thought they had an understanding. Elvis realized his mistake the night she told him she thought she was pregnant.

"You told me it was the wrong time of the month for that," Elvis blurted in exasperation.

"I guess I was wrong. I'm not positive, but I'm hardly ever late. If you were so concerned, you should of used a rubber," she smiled, snuggling against him in his car, where they had just made love, parked down the street from her house. Elvis enjoyed the urgency and risk of having sex in a public place, but her announcement shattered his reverie.

Elvis was in a state of disbelief—he had never anticipated this with any woman—and gave a little laugh. She kissed him and held him tight, while he could only say, "Oh, baby." She mistook his shocked expression and frozen smile for joy and climbed out of the car excited and happy. Elvis drove to his hotel, trying to figure out what to do, but the thoughts muddled in his head: *What would Mama say ... it'd kill her ... why now ... how could he support two more mouths ... how could he keep singing ... why did bad things always happen to him?*

Elvis didn't answer his phone at all the next day and tried avoiding her after his performance the following night by slipping out the back. She was waiting for him, angry and crying, at his motel door when he finally got there, the smell of cheap perfume clinging to him. Her tears softened him up, and he comforted her until she wanted to know if he didn't want to marry her; then he panicked all over again.

"You gotta be crazy. I don't wanna get married. I can't."

"You said you loved me," she wailed. "What am I supposed to do about our baby?"

"You're not sure you are pregnant." Elvis pushed her away with a hard set to his face. "Besides, how would I even know it's *our* baby? If you whore around with me, Lord knows who else you whore around with when I ain't here. It could be anybody's kid, and I ain't taking the rap for it."

She walked up to Elvis and slapped him hard across the face. "My daddy always told me not to get involved with trash. I should have listened."

Fear and anger and panic boiled over. He grabbed her arm and dragged her to the door. "At least I ain't no whore. You probably ain't pregnant at all, just using it as an excuse to get me to marry you. I'm sick of lying, cheating women. Get the hell outta here." He slammed the door behind her and turned the radio up full blast to drown out her crying outside the door. He hated himself for making her cry, but what else could he do? He couldn't stop now, not when he was so close. He lay on the bed with the pillow over his face, tears wetting the coarse cotton. He'd come so far and hadn't gone anywhere. He was still screwing up every way he turned.

He didn't hear from her again, and more than once he had to resist the urge to drive by her house. He wondered if she had been pregnant but was too afraid to find out. He justified his actions by convincing himself that she was just trying to use him to get away from her family. Elvis breathed a deep sigh of relief when his stint at the Louisiana Hayride was history.

Chapter 9

BREAKING THROUGH

Through his connections, Parker arranged bookings for Elvis at larger venues in the South, including an eight-day tour in Texas with Ferlin Husky. Husky was a somewhat eccentric performer who developed a more comedic and less psychotic Andy Kaufman–esque alter ego named Simon Crum. All the while, Parker was doing just enough to propel Elvis along, but keeping his full plan a secret—he wasn't about to share in the ultimate success with anyone. He was content to bide his time.

Thanks to Parker, Elvis's third single, "Baby, Let's Play House," was his first record to make the national country charts. Everybody celebrated the breakthrough, but the festivities were strained—it was clear there were too many cooks in the kitchen. The Colonel and Neal disagreed on virtually everything: where Elvis should be playing, what songs he should be singing, and most of all, what label he should be on.

Parker confided to Vernon with a shrug. "I'm trying to help the kid, but Neal's tying my hands. Tell Elvis I'll do my best, but I don't think I can do anything more for him at this rate. Getting on the national charts isn't that tough—but staying there is. I'd hate for Elvis to be a flash-in-the-pan because of an ignorant manager."

By the look of panic on Vernon's face, the Colonel knew it was time to make his next move. A shrewd businessman, Parker took Elvis, Gladys, and Vernon to a classy restaurant, tasteful but not too expensive. He didn't want to come across as extravagant, just cultured. An expert name-dropper, he impressed them with stories about the likes of Carl Perkins, Hank Williams, and Jerry Lee Lewis.

After dessert, Parker finally put his cards on the table. During his time with Arnold, he'd been able to develop solid national contacts. He knew how to deal with record companies and promised Elvis he could have him signed with a top label in a matter of weeks, because he knew the ins and outs of contract law and was personal friends with many music industry executives.

He convinced them that his contacts and knowledge of the way big business was played were two assets invaluable to a struggling performer like Elvis. He told them in a chilling voice that the difference between him and Bob Neal was the difference between success and failure, security or the return to poverty. Parker played on Elvis's most profound fears, and they proved to be his trump cards.

Back home, the Presleys had a long family conference. Vernon was all for Parker and said they never should have gone with Neal in the first place. Gladys was unable to explain her strong mistrust of Parker to Elvis, who wasn't 100 percent sure himself. Change always filled Elvis with anxiety, and in this case, loyalties clouded the issue even more.

"I don't wanna be disrespectful to Bob or Mr. Phillips. I can't forget about them."

"He's right, Vernon," Gladys agreed. "And at least we know we can trust Bob and Sam."

Vernon thought they were being naïve. "It's about business, Mama, not who's likable. Son, Bob'll understand; he won't stand in your way. He did what he could now it's time to move on. You'd be making a big mistake not giving Parker a chance."

"But he also talked about dropping Sun. I don't think I can do that to Mr. Phillips."

The discussion raged back and forth for hours, a tortured process for Elvis, who wanted to do what was right but was driven by the desire to be somebody. When Vernon brought up legal and money matters and what it would take to buy out his Sun contract, Elvis threw himself down on the couch with disgust.

"I wish I understood half of what was going on."

"Which is why you need someone like Parker," reasoned Vernon. "He's the big time. None of us here are capable of handling it, but he is. And don't you forget it."

It was one of the few times Elvis let Vernon get so involved in a decision, and Vernon finally convinced Elvis to make the change. Truth be told, Elvis's nightmare was that he would wake up in 20 years to find himself still playing the same clubs. Once Elvis agreed, Gladys reluctantly went along with the decision. Hating confrontation, Elvis let Vernon make the call to Bob Neal.

Later, Elvis met up with Earl and told him what had happened over fries and a milkshake. He was still troubled by his decision and the uncertainty of it.

"I don't know if I'm doing the right thing," he admitted. "Colonel Parker says I can make it really big, but to do that, I gotta leave Sun for a bigger record company. I feel worse about that than I do for Bob. If it weren't for Mr. Phillips, I'd still be driving a truck. "It's funny ... I love singing, and when I'm up on stage, it feels so good but the rest of it can make you feel pretty bad."

Elvis signed with Parker, agreeing to pay him 25 percent of his earnings, an unusually high fee. But within a few months the Colonel swung the deal that saw RCA buy out the remaining year of Elvis's Sun contract for $35,000—with a $5,000 bonus going to Elvis.

He showed Earl the check, and they just stared at it for a long, long time. The money gave Elvis the freedom to start enjoying the luxuries he had only fantasized about, such as buying his first complete outfit at Lansky Brothers and taking girls out on fancy dates. Some of his big nights out were disappointing. After trying two or three of Memphis's highly touted restaurants, Elvis decided he preferred the taste of real food served by people who didn't look down their noses at you if you used the wrong fork. He'd still take a girl to a nice place to impress her, but on his way home in the wee hours of the morning, he'd stop at an all-night diner for a greasy cheeseburger.

Elvis was most excited about the gift he got for his family: he rented a furnished house on Getwell Drive and moved his parents into their first real home. Gladys was so overwhelmed she got flushed and felt faint. "Maybe we ought to go back to the other place," Elvis teased her when she revived. In response, Gladys hugged Elvis for dear life, soaking his shirt with her tears. Even Vernon was misty-eyed when he walked into the clean-smelling, brightly lit, modest home in a neighborhood that had grass and trees.

They were like kids let loose in a toy store, wide-eyed and unable to believe their good fortune—Elvis especially. But beneath the giddiness he felt an occasional flash of worry. For the first time in his life, Elvis actually had something to lose. It made him even more determined to work hard and do everything Parker said. After all, he had arranged for the bonus in the first place.

Vernon thought Parker was a gift from God, a wise sage who would lead them to the promised land of riches. But even sitting in her new home,

Gladys still thought Parker was a hustler and someone to keep an eye on. Not even the gifts he continually sent her helped diminish her unease. Elvis didn't have strong feelings about him one way or another; he was just glad to have someone to handle confusing business matters and who could make him money. "Hey, I'll stick with anyone who makes me rich," he would say.

Partly because of Gladys's dislike of Parker and partly because Elvis himself wasn't totally comfortable with his company, the relationship with Parker stayed very much business. He wasn't invited over for dinner, nor did Elvis ever consider him a buddy. The only one who went out of his way to be chummy was Vernon, which was another strike against Parker as far as Elvis was concerned. But the bottom line was business—Elvis wanted to be famous and he wanted to have money, and he'd do almost anything to have both.

Elvis drove his car around town as if he owned the streets. He wanted to show off his good fortune to everyone he had ever felt insignificant next to, except it still didn't make him any more secure inside. Initially, at least, it gave him pleasure to think he had something over other people and made him feel like a big shot. And to cover his fear of losing that edge, he adopted a cocky demeanor, except around Gladys. He now knew she wouldn't tolerate a smart mouth or a patronizing attitude, no matter how much money he had in the bank. So at home, he was the same old Elvis. But when he was out, he became a swaggering Mr. Cool.

When Gladys saw this side of him in performance, her face crinkled in concern and her hands worried the hem of her dress. She silently blamed Parker for corrupting her boy.

Parker had told Elvis he needed to sharpen his stage presence and develop an image; specifically, he needed to play up his sexuality and make both the men and the women in the audience want him. The erotic reference to men shocked Elvis, but it intrigued him at the same time. He'd never felt comfortable around men and had only begun to feel comfortable around women when he learned to "overpower" them with sex. The idea that he could control men the same way—not by sleeping with them but by daring them not to notice his sexual smolder—had never occurred to him, until Parker brought it up. He found the thought of being wanted by a man oddly erotic, and it made him feel powerful and superior.

The only problem was that Elvis felt uncomfortable acting this out in front of Gladys, so he began to gently discourage her from attending his performances at the nicer clubs, which were the only ones she'd attend. He'd tell her he had businesspeople to meet and wouldn't be able to spend time with her. "It's just for now," he promised. "Once things get going good, we'll have lots of time together."

Elvis worked hard at the clubs and on the road dates Parker arranged, preparing for his first record with his new label. He couldn't afford any disasters—this time he'd get only one chance, and if he blew it, he'd lose it all. The family was solely his responsibility. Since his signing and getting the bonus, both his parents quit working, citing health reasons; the pressure was on.

It had been only a little more than two years since he had graduated from high school and started driving a truck, but it seemed a lifetime ago. Time had passed in a flash, with the nights on the road and in the clubs with the dozens of faceless women merging together into an indistinct flurry of images.

So much had changed in such a short period of time. Here he was on the verge of realizing a dream, and yet when he was alone, an unexplained melancholy would come over him. Sometimes he wondered about Dixie, hoping she knew what she was missing. But even that wish of measured revenge left him more empty than satisfied.

He felt curiously removed from a lot of the whirlwind surrounding him, except when he was on stage performing. It wasn't just the singing that he loved—it was singing for someone. Even during rehearsals, he played to his musicians or whoever happened to be around, and he fed off the response.

Two years earlier, he'd thought that if he could make enough money singing so that Gladys wouldn't have to work and they could move to a nicer place, he'd be happy. Success was supposed to solve all of one's problems. But despite everything he'd achieved, he still felt the same inside. Sure, he was pleased and enjoyed the attention and notoriety, but when he was quiet and alone, he still felt an ache, an emptiness—he just hadn't accomplished enough. So he set his sights on making more money and being famous everywhere in the country, not just his region of the South. He was convinced that reaching this goal would make him happy and content. He was counting on Parker to work his magic, and that's why he agreed to pay the Colonel almost half of what he was earning. Meanwhile, Elvis was so busy looking ahead that he was missing out on the present.

In January 1956, after a lot of persuasive campaigning by Parker, *Cashbox* named Elvis the best new country-and-western artist of 1955. That same month, his first RCA single, "Heartbreak Hotel," zoomed to number one. Within a matter of a few weeks all hell broke loose, and the life he'd previously known was gone forever.

A whirlwind of activity suddenly surrounded Elvis as the record company cranked the publicity machine into high gear to cash in on the popularity of "Heartbreak Hotel." While fans of all ages flocked to buy his records, he was a hit particularly with teenagers and young adults, just as Parker had foreseen. He knew Elvis would have a limited and brief career if he didn't break out in a drastically new direction, and he waited for the perfect time to launch his plan.

Elvis was neither true country nor a contemporary of the Doris Day–Eddie Fisher–Pat Boone style of music. He was a performer who spoke directly to his peers, and youth was the wave of the future. Others would come around in time, but it was the teens and the young adults who would usher Elvis in on a throne, due to more than sheer talent.

The fifties had been a decade of conservatism and repression. Uniformity and not rocking the boat were ideals to live by, but the social claustrophobia of such a structured climate had the restless young in the country actively looking for their own identity—an identity as far removed from "I like Ike" as they could find. They were looking for someone like Elvis, whose unique singing and dancing style, tailored hair, and bad-boy sexuality oozed rebellion and a break from the mundane. Elvis blew in on a breath of fresh air, and Parker was there to meet him and market him for all he was worth.

Elvis was an overnight sensation for most of the country and tumbled into the spotlight unprepared for its glare. Photo sessions were set up, and Elvis posed for hours under hot lights, trying to smolder on cue for the camera. Even though he was the music world's newest sensation, Elvis was intimidated by the impatient photographers who took roll after roll of pictures while he tried to relax enough to get it right. He covered his nervousness with jokes and banter, but kept his shaking hands in his pockets. He finally asked for a radio to be turned on, and with music as his guide, he was able to strike the poses and catch the look.

Label publicists sat with Elvis and tried to hammer out an acceptable, antiseptic biography. Vernon and Gladys were particularly worried that Vernon's checkered past would surface, so Elvis was reluctantly forced to confide in Parker about his family's prior troubles. The Colonel assured Elvis that nobody would find out, and he filed the information away for his own future use.

With requests for print interviews and TV appearances flooding in, Parker gave Elvis a crash course in how to meet the press and the public. Whenever possible, he got a publication to submit its questions first so he could coach Elvis on the answers. When a particular magazine or newspaper wouldn't agree, Parker would carefully remind Elvis to think over the question twice, speak slowly, and be friendly. To make sure all went smoothly, Parker hovered nearby, ready to interrupt if the direction of the interview took a dangerous turn. Elvis was grateful for Parker's protection and accepted the unspoken conclusion that without the Colonel, he would be lost.

Parker cleverly encouraged that dependency by playing on Elvis's obvious insecurities. He would explain a business matter or performance agreement in the most technical of terms, knowing full well it was confusing the hell out of Elvis. When Elvis didn't understand, Parker would pat him on the back and tell him not to worry about it: "You just let me handle it. You take care of the singing."

The subtly patronizing tone made Elvis feel like an incapable, dumb little kid, which further eroded his already fragile self-confidence. Frustrated and convinced he'd never be smart enough to understand the business end of his career, he stopped trying. He turned it over to Parker completely, saying he didn't even want to hear any of it—such as how even though Bob Neal had a contract that ran until March 1956, he had been dumped months before and got no share of the RCA money.

Instead, Elvis immersed himself in the luxury of popularity and the excitement of being wanted by everybody. He fed off this public outpouring, especially from the fans who started surrounding him when he went out. Through it all, though, the best feeling was still being up on stage, singing to his people and basking in the love they sent back.

The Colonel understood media and he understood crowds. Newspapers were more apt to give preferential coverage to someone who created the biggest stir. Elvis's performances quickly gained notoriety after the release of "Heartbreak Hotel," because of the near hysteria he caused among his fans. Parker ensured early crowd reaction by paying dozens of young girls to start the screaming that would spread like wildfire through the audience.

Mob psychology is fascinating—and predictable. Get one group yelling and pushing its way to the front, and everybody gets caught up in the swell. It wasn't honest, but it was a brilliant strategy.

Elvis's sensuality stirred the dormant fifties libido, and the Colonel was marketing this side of Elvis even more than his singing. His eyes held the promise of ecstasy, but at the same time, the vulnerability that was Elvis still shone through. The combination was irresistible. He was a consummate stage performer, and every member of that audience, man and woman, felt he was reaching out just to him or her. And each one of them reached back.

Gladys was appalled at Elvis's provocative image and the reaction it caused. Even if she didn't see him perform much anymore, she was aware of the girls following him around, eyeing him with blatant invitation.

While Elvis left his image at the door when he was home, Gladys could still sense a change in him. There was a jauntiness she found troubling, because she associated it with insincerity. She dreaded the thought of Elvis turning into one of those smooth-talking men with the shifty eyes—like Parker. She was grateful for Elvis's sudden, mind-boggling success, but was afraid he had made a deal with the devil to get it.

Gladys would have been convinced had she known what Elvis did when he was away from her on the road. The higher his song went on the national Top 40 charts, the bigger the selection of women. Even though Elvis was drawn to classy, sophisticated women, they were too intimidating to pursue. Instead, he turned his attention to the barflies and groupies, easy marks who were more open to suggestions, such as having sex in the car while parked on a public street or sharing his bed with another woman.

Elvis first discovered the thrill of sleeping with two women while on tour in Texas and tried to repeat the experience every chance he got. Parker didn't care about Elvis's sexual habits as long as he was discreet. "Put up a good front in public, and you'll be free to do what you want in private," Parker counseled. "Just don't mix them up."

The transformation from a sexy, libidinous singing star on the road to a mama's boy at home was stressful. At times he resented Gladys's constant supervision and questions, wishing for the freedom he felt away from her. But as soon as he entertained thoughts of being on his own, he was overcome by a stabbing guilt. How could he even consider shutting her out after all she'd sacrificed for him? So at home he reverted back to the dutiful son and kept his other life tucked away like a secret diary.

Even so, Gladys sensed Elvis was heading down a dangerous path, and the urge to hover over him was stronger than ever. She was honest enough to admit she wasn't smart enough to go head to head with big businessmen—neither was Elvis. They were suddenly at the mercy of strangers, and it scared her.

Gladys also resented having to share Elvis with so many others. She was painfully proud of him, but she desperately wanted her little boy back and the time they used to share together. For all the money and clothes and jewelry, she was lonelier and more neglected than she'd ever been in her life. She didn't want presents; she wanted time and affection. Gladys's only comfort was the bottle, and she turned to it with a vengeance. But Elvis was so busy trying to adjust to all the demands on his time, he simply didn't have enough left over.

Within weeks of bursting onto the scene with "Heartbreak Hotel," Elvis was scheduled to appear on his first national TV show, Tommy and

Jimmy Dorsey's *The Stage Show*, which broadcast from Manhattan. Even though Elvis's appearance was well received, New York again succeeded in taking some of the wind out of his sails. The city made him nervous and antsy, uncomfortable with the cosmopolitan people, and desperately homesick. This was one road he didn't want to stay on. He called Gladys every night, keeping her on the phone far longer than he did when he and his combo were playing the dusty clubs of the South. He was a fish out of water in New York and was convinced people were secretly making fun of him. "If I hear one more person talk about my 'cute' accent, I'm gonna pop 'em," he warned her.

Elvis was angrier at some reporters in a press conference who accused him of corrupting the morals of the nation's youth with his suggestive stage gyrations. "It's not on purpose," he tried to explain. "That's just the way I sing best. I gotta feel the music. It's just singing and that don't hurt anyone."

Except for performing, Elvis enjoyed talking to the fans the best, signing autographs and posing for pictures with the "regular" people who loved him and his music. But the industry people he met made him feel inconsequential, and he disliked them for it. In public, Elvis buried his resentments and was gracious, accommodating, and polite, but back at the hotel, he'd sulk. Elvis was expert at hiding his true emotions, particularly around people in authority. He'd swallow his bile and be a good boy to their face, then rage and sputter when they left. He was simply repeating and perfecting the way he had dealt with Vernon over the years.

Elvis knew he should be eternally grateful for being in this position, but success still didn't feel the way it was supposed to.

Chapter 10

LIGHTS, CAMERA, ACTION

In the spring of 1956, Parker arranged for Elvis to appear in Las Vegas at the New Frontier Hotel. Even though Elvis had been traveling over a solid year, Las Vegas was something more than just another road show. It was the showplace of the world where major performers strutted their talent. It told Elvis he had truly arrived, and scared him to death. Typically, his defense mechanisms transformed his excitement into complaints and worry—if he expected the worst, he wouldn't be disappointed when it happened.

Las Vegas unsettled Elvis, but in a different way than New York had. Elvis was the new kid on the strip and hated the familiar feeling of being on the outside looking in. Not that the other performers he met weren't warm, but there was a professional distance. He tensed under their scrutiny as his insecurities bubbled to the surface. He wilted under the examination and retreated into himself and his room.

On the other hand, there was a lot about Vegas that appealed to Elvis and made him feel comfortable. He enjoyed the constant activity of the casinos, filled with people around the clock, and the lively sound of money changing hands. The fashions of Vegas—sequined jackets and clingy materials in bright colors—matched his own loud preferences.

Elvis sneaked out on his own long after Parker assumed he was asleep. Wearing a hat to hide his telltale hair, he cruised the local bars to recharge his sagging batteries, the rowdy nightlife comforting and familiar. He'd bring one or more women back to his hotel and keep room service jumping with orders of champagne for the ladies and oysters for himself. Elvis often had trouble sleeping, and being awake at dawn made him melancholy, so the party would end before sunrise. After an all-night romp, he was worn out enough to immediately fall asleep.

Elvis attracted a large audience at the casino, and although they were less vocal than his teenage fans, it was still a very successful appearance. Among the people watching Elvis with special interest was Hal Wallis, a Hollywood film producer. Wallis knew that many singers had made a successful and profitable transition to film, including Doris Day and Pat Boone. He suspected the camera would love Elvis, with his bedroom eyes and little-boy vulnerability. Parker greeted Wallis warmly but was non-committal, letting the producer believe others had already made offers.

But for as good as Parker was, Wallis was better. He was clever enough and secure enough to let the Colonel believe it was he who had the upper hand. The bottom line was most important to Wallis. After all the lunging and parrying were over, Elvis flew to Los Angeles for a screen test and was back in Vegas before dinnertime to catch the next train home.

He was happy to be back in Memphis and put the movies out of his mind, too wrapped up in the pride of buying his family their own home to think of much else. The house was on Audubon Drive, a quiet, middle-class neighborhood with nicely kept lawns; neat, freshly painted homes; and nervous neighbors who greeted the Presleys hesitantly. Having a famous and controversial singer living next door worried the residents of Audubon Drive, especially when his family appeared to be something straight out of a Ma and Pa Kettle movie. Their first impressions were justified.

The house was filled with new furniture that didn't match, in colors that hurt the eyes. Gladys's true pride and joy, though, was the flower-trimmed backyard, where she planned to raise chickens.

She loved her new home with all its luxuries, but she was also desperate to hold on to a familiar way of life. It didn't occur to her that their neighbors might not appreciate being hooted out of bed at dawn by a cock's crowing. Nor did Elvis see anything wrong with having chickens and a rooster in the middle of a city.

Colonel Parker couldn't tell the Presleys what to do in their own home, but it was his job to avert any public disasters. It was imperative that the whole Presley family be prepared for the demands of success, no matter how inconvenient. When the Colonel sat them down to give them pointers on dealing with the press, Vernon was amenable, but Gladys resented any intrusion by Parker. Her feathers were immediately ruffled as he counseled them on everything from answering questions to their appearance.

Elvis recruited Earl to handle some of his personal business, like writing letters and organizing his fan mail. One day Elvis was sitting at the table signing a stack of photographs when he suddenly remembered to mention that his old high school classmate Red West had stopped by.

Earl suggested he hire Red to answer the front door, now that so many people were knocking on it hoping to meet Elvis. "You're famous and need to start being more careful," Earl told him. "And get a higher fence, so they just can't step over it like they do now."

"Be more careful of those girls? I can handle 'em."

"It's not girls—it's their boyfriends."

Elvis took the joke very seriously. "Maybe I *ought* to think about giving Red something to do. He's a big guy ... maybe he could be a bodyguard when I'm out performing."

Elvis was going to need a bodyguard at home, too. The people living on either side of the Presleys were upset about the number of cars driving past, the noise, the crowds of girls encamped on the sidewalk, and the general disruption of home life as they'd known it.

They were also appalled at what they saw when they looked over their back fences: stacks of wood littered the corner where Gladys intended to build her coop, plus she had clothesline strung every which way so she could hang her laundry out to dry, daily. This neighborhood preferred not to see drying underwear spanning the entire backyard, high above the fence sightline.

Despite complaints, Elvis wasn't about to compromise, or to tell Gladys she had to change anything in her own house and yard. He made matters worse by refusing to even discuss the problems, nor was he about to alter his aversion of confrontation. The hostility grew on both sides, and soon the Presleys were the outcasts of a block that couldn't have cared less if he was a star. No longer whispering, they spoke cruel words loudly over morning coffee and backyard hedges.

Elvis got so angry at hearing himself and his family being called white trash again, he stormed out to the backyard and broke several two-by-fours, littering the grass even more. It was beyond him why anyone would be upset, and he decided the neighbors were simply jealous.

In July 1956, Elvis was riding atop the charts with "Don't Be Cruel" and "Hound Dog." His popularity was at a fever pitch, and his first album was on its way to selling a million copies—a feat never before accomplished. The money was rolling in, and it burned a hole in Elvis's pocket. He bought a dozen more outfits from Lansky's and bought Gladys a pink Cadillac—even though she hated to drive.

Elvis gave in to his desire to show off his wealth every chance he got, in an attempt to prove his worth and value as a person to those who still considered him trash. In public, he was still polite and upbeat, but in private he would suffer through sharp mood swings. Sometimes he felt so worthless it was hard for him to remember how famous he was.

Women were the best support for his sagging ego, and he would go out at night looking for someone to soothe his soul and release the building pressure. But even this was more complicated now. Elvis was an idol, and he was news. He eyed with desire the young girls who followed him, but he had to be careful where he was seen and with whom, unless he wanted Gladys to read about it in the morning papers. He pouted at not being able to use his wealth and fame the way he wanted.

His attitude in the recording studio was changing as well. He wasn't as eager to please and, knowing he was the star, often showed up late and unprepared. It gave him a feeling of power to keep people waiting and know they'd still be there when he arrived. However, when he got to the studio he was full of down-home apologies and good humor, so his antics were forgiven.

Parker worked him hard during rehearsals, concentrating on stage presence and preparation. Elvis had a terrible memory and often forgot the words to a song, which could spell disaster on TV. When he'd muff his lines during a live performance, Elvis covered up by dancing his wild gyrations. Half the time when he broke into the swiveling that made him famous, it was merely because he had forgotten the words, and dancing gave him time to gather his thoughts. Other times, if the crowd was especially noisy and raucous, he'd just make up words as he went along.

Parker wanted Elvis relaxed but not that loose. He stressed the importance of being professional. It was fine to have fun, but in a disciplined way. The tutoring wore Elvis out, but he followed Parker's instructions and doggedly worked on memorization exercises and improving his stage presence. The last thing he wanted was to make a fool of himself in front of the fans who mattered so much to him.

That summer, when he wasn't in the recording studio working on his singing or on the road touring, Elvis was taking diction lessons at Parker's insistence. Elvis was about to take an important step in his career, and Parker knew there might not be any second chances if Elvis blew it the first time around. Hal Wallis had made good on his word and signed Elvis to star in his first movie. Originally, it was going to be called *Reno Brothers*, but Paramount Studios changed it to *Love Me Tender* to capitalize on his latest hit single.

Initially, Elvis had balked and was insulted that Parker insist he take diction lessons. He saw nothing wrong with the way he spoke and was adamant that he wasn't going to do it. Parker eyed Elvis with an unblinking stare. "I'm sure your mama would be very upset to know you'd rather be out fooling with not one but two girls at a time like you did in Las Vegas, instead of being serious about your career. It might break her heart, wouldn't it?"

The argument was immediately over. After Parker left, Elvis went out back, furious and frightened. He vented his frustration by throwing lawn chairs around, shocked to realize that Parker had been spying on him.

But his indignation was quickly doused as the thought of *acting* in a movie sank in. Elvis was overwhelmed and terrified. He had no training as an actor and doubted a crash course would help much. In front of his musicians and instructors, Elvis covered his fear with bravado, but alone at night in bed, he hugged his pillow and prayed for Jesse to make everything all right.

With Parker a stern taskmaster, Elvis worked diligently to prepare himself for the next phase of his career. Elvis regarded the Colonel warily, and while they had never been buddies, a new coolness and distance separated them. When it was finally time to go, Elvis joked that he looked forward to going to California to work so that he could get some rest.

Unless it was absolutely necessary, Elvis refused to get on an airplane, so he and Earl went to Los Angeles by train; Parker, Vernon, and Gladys would follow later. After a hectic final week and Gladys's frantic and tearful goodbyes, Elvis sank into his seat with a relieved sigh. He couldn't shake the worry that Parker would "tell" on him, and he hoped the trip would make it go away.

As the train pulled out of the station, Elvis was excited and jumpy, unable to sit still. He wasn't able to find any suitable female companionship, so he spent the trip going over his script and practicing his pronunciation. Being alone with his childhood friend allowed Elvis to relax and not worry about living up to anyone's expectations.

For Earl, though, it was bittersweet. "Seeing his old self again reminded me more than ever how so much about Elvis had changed, and how different he was now. He'd become so distrustful of people in such a short period of time—in his mind they either wanted to make him look bad or were laughing behind his back or jealous. He couldn't see it was his own insecurities that haunted him. He was so adept at hiding his true feelings that it was inevitable they would erupt in an uncontrollable way at some point in time."

Once on the set, Elvis wasn't very interested in the process of making movies. Artistically, he thought it was pretty silly, although he admitted he was having fun and enjoyed seeing himself on film. Much of Elvis's ease was due to his beautiful costar, Debra Paget, whom he started falling for. Visions of romance replaced images of raw passion, and he pictured her in his home, sharing his life. When he sang to her in the movie, the feeling behind the words was genuine.

The studio kept Elvis hopping from dawn to dusk. When he was done filming for the day, Elvis might go for more publicity photos, do an interview, or attend a function with Debra. Even though he didn't like going to public functions, being with Debra made it bearable. He couldn't be alone with her much because of their busy shooting and publicity schedule, and because Gladys was always close by. He talked to Debra on the phone every night, shutting himself in his bedroom so he didn't have to hear Gladys's pointed sighing.

Parker dragged Elvis to a number of parties, sometimes accompanied by Debra, sometimes alone. He didn't want Elvis linked to any one person and made sure he had his photograph taken with a lot of different starlets. Many people were eager to meet Elvis, especially a young actress named Natalie Wood. Elvis was attracted to her dark, pretty looks and innocent air, and he was impressed that someone like her would seek him out. On a whim he invited her to Memphis, never believing she'd take him up on it.

His crush on Natalie blossomed simultaneously as his obsession with Debra faded. His change of heart was colored by the realization that his costar didn't want him as a boyfriend or even a brief lover. He had only tried to kiss her, too respectful to suggest anything else, and had been shocked—and angry—at her rebuff. Elvis couldn't fathom the idea that a man and a woman could just be friends. "You can't be friends with women, not like buddies. It don't work."

By the time the movie was finished, Elvis was ready to go home to the familiar streets of Memphis. As soon as they arrived, Elvis jumped into his car and picked up some cheeseburgers at Leonard's, where he rekindled an old flirtation with his favorite carhop.

Memphis recharged Elvis and lightened his burden of unfulfilled expectations, which is why he would always call Memphis home. It was his safety valve and retreat, a place to salve the wounds and heal the bruises of feeling knocked in the press and snubbed by those who acted superior. Elvis was the biggest fish in this pond, more accepted here than anywhere by people who reminded him time and again why singing was so important. In Memphis he would always be second to none, the king beloved by his minions.

NATIONAL ICON

In September, Parker pulled off his biggest coup to date—a booking on the *Ed Sullivan Show*. What made it especially sweet was that Sullivan had previously announced he would *never* invite Elvis and his swiveling hips on the show. Viewer pressure made Sullivan eat his words, but he refused to admit complete defeat and would only let the cameramen shoot Elvis from the waist up, lest he corrupt the morals of young girls everywhere. Elvis's truncated performance became part of television history and firmly established the boy from Memphis as the most popular performer in America. He was only 23 years old.

Elvis used to find it funny when he was warned about his personal safety, but a tense moment in the week following the *Sullivan* appearance scared him into reality. Elvis returned home from a rehearsal session and noticed a crowd of fans in front of his house. He was tired, but he still enjoyed talking to fans and signing autographs. He stepped out of his car and walked toward the group. A couple of young girls started screaming and made a mad rush toward Elvis, causing the other fans to do the same thing. He attempted to get back inside his car, but he wasn't quick enough, and they literally pinned Elvis against the hood. Their combined weight crushed against him and scared the hell out of him when he found it hard to take complete breaths. He tried to push his way out from their grasp, but there were too many of them, and his panic turned to terror.

Suddenly, the crowd began to let up and Elvis saw his dad and Uncle Vester (Vernon's brother who had married Gladys's sister Cletis) pulling kids away. Elvis had never in his whole life been so happy to see his father. Vernon grabbed him by both arms and took him into the house, with Vester still holding the crowd back with a menacing two-by-four.

Elvis couldn't stop shaking and huddled in Gladys's arms, thinking about what might have happened if she had been with him. The fright might have literally given her a heart attack. Parker had warned him this would happen, but Elvis thought he was just talking to hear himself, as usual. But now Elvis realized he had to make some changes to protect both himself and his family.

The first thing Elvis did was hire Red West to be his personal bodyguard. Although just Red was on the payroll in the beginning, Elvis encouraged West to bring around buddies to tag along on excursions out. For the first time in his life, he had a group of male friends to pal around with, and he relished being the leader of the pack.

Elvis felt safe with Red, but he knew his living arrangements weren't suitable anymore. Besides wanting a house with less public access, he craved more room so he could go outside and clear his mind; the days of taking walks in the neighborhood were over forever. Elvis also coveted stature. He wanted a home that made a statement about who he was and how far he'd come, a place where nobody—neighbors included—could interfere with his life. He found the home of his dreams at an estate named Graceland.

Elvis and Gladys spent several full days in some of the city's most expensive stores picking out furniture, wallpaper, and paint for their new home. Gladys was in her glory—not because of the house, but because of the time Elvis was spending with her. But once the shopping was done and they were settled in their new home, Elvis turned his time and attention elsewhere, and she sank back into melancholy. The only difference was she now drank in beautiful surroundings.

Elvis was constantly on the go. When he wasn't performing, he was rehearsing and recording. Once his business obligations for the day were done, Elvis concentrated on enjoying himself. On the road, he would cruise clubs with Red for women. At home in Memphis, Elvis lived out an adolescent fantasy. He rented out movie theaters to watch private showings, and he paid the owner of his favorite amusement arcade to stay open after hours for him to play pinball and other games of chance until dawn.

Elvis preferred the cover of night, the darkness enabling him to move around with slightly greater freedom. But staying up until all hours meant he often didn't go to bed until it was nearly dawn. Parker accommodated him by arranging for his rehearsals and recording sessions to be held later in the day, so Elvis got into the habit of sleeping past noon.

At least once a week when he was in town, Elvis would rent out the Rainbow Roller Rink for $75 a night. He would tell Red to get together a nice-sized group, and they would go skating, sometimes until dawn. On all these excursions, Elvis was surrounded by a small group of buddies who began to wear their hair as he did and to dress as he did; although at this point, the only constant face was Red's.

Once at Graceland, Elvis never strayed out of the house unaccompanied. Safety aside, a group of buddies acted as a buffer. For as much as he loved attention, Elvis hated feeling he was under scrutiny, and he found the line between the two getting hazier as time went on. Eating in restaurants became an ordeal, as other patrons stared at him constantly or whispered about him in hushed tones.

Elvis sometimes felt overwhelmed by the pressure of etiquette. Learning why you were given two forks and two glasses at a table setting was bad enough, but remembering not to put your elbows on the table, or tuck the napkin into your shirt collar, or wad your napkin into a ball on your plate when you were done eating was plain boring. But Parker harped on him about it and shamed him into paying attention by reminding him that people would think he was an uncouth hillbilly. It was an effort to remember everything, and as a result, at home he rebelled and made it a point to be as "uncouth" as he wanted to be.

Chapter 11

LOSS

Elvis hadn't had a steady girlfriend since Dixie. Natalie Wood had been little more than a fling, a hurried coupling in the back of a limo. He showed Natalie his Memphis—with private roller skating parties, his merry band of men, and his adoring fans—but was disappointed that she wasn't really impressed.

Then Anita Wood came into his life. She was a local celebrity from hosting the TV show *Dance Party*. One afternoon while flipping through the channels, Elvis saw her and decided right then and there he had to go out with her. He had one of his guys call. Anita was flattered but made it clear she wasn't going out with anyone who couldn't call her himself. Eventually, Elvis did call, and the lively, pretty blonde became his primary girlfriend, although he refused to be exclusive with her and said up front they should both be free to see others.

Vernon liked Anita and thought Elvis should be grateful to find a lady of her caliber interested in him. He thought Elvis an idiot for not settling down immediately with her, but Anita seemed to accept their relationship.

Although Elvis was constantly surrounded by his gang of guys, the only people he completely trusted were his parents; Vernon's mother, Miss Minnie, whom he had moved to Graceland from West Point, Mississippi; Red West; Earl; and Alberta, the maid Gladys had hired while they were still on Audubon Drive. Alberta was too down-to-earth to be impressed, shocked, or bothered by much, so she and Elvis hit it off immediately. He got a kick out of her honesty and knew she would treat him the same regardless of whether he was rich or poor. It was ironic that the more successful Elvis became, the more he sought out simple people—the kind he had left behind in Tupelo as a boy.

Elvis was on top of the world, but there were already warning signs that his paranoia was growing. Everyone knew Elvis could be stubborn and Elvis had a temper, but he shocked everyone over an incident with Anita.

He had bought Anita a beautiful ring that she treasured, one he picked out himself and had custom designed. A few weeks later on *Dance Party,* Anita was on the stage singing a song when the cameraman zoomed in for a close-up of the ring on her hand. Elvis was watching and when he saw the ring filling the picture tube, he became enraged.

Vernon, Red, and Earl looked on, stunned, as he ranted about her taking advantage of him. Vernon came to her defense, but Elvis refused to be mollified. Although he and Anita continued to date, it was a worrisome example of Elvis's skewed reality.

By the summer of 1958, Elvis was too busy for any relationship. He was in the recording studio nonstop until it was time to leave for Hollywood to star in his third film, *Kid Creole.* The novelty of making movies had already worn off; on the whole, Elvis was pretty bored, especially since no costar had caught his eye for a set romance.

Paramount put Elvis up at the posh Beverly Wilshire Hotel. Elvis drove room service crazy ordering cheeseburgers at all hours. For breakfast he insisted they make him a fried peanut-butter-and-banana sandwich, even though it meant the hotel had to send a runner out for peanut butter. He was eager to finish the film so he could get back to Memphis and have a little fun. But those plans—and a whole lot more—were shot to hell when Parker called.

Elvis had been drafted.

He didn't take the news well. Feeling as if the bottom had just fallen out of his world, Elvis, crying and cursing, yanked open the window and started throwing pieces of furniture onto the parking lot below. Parker immediately called the draft board and got a deferment that enabled Elvis to finish his movie and then return to Memphis for a few weeks. Elvis was still numb and Gladys cried as Parker explained why Elvis needed to report for duty rather than try to get into Special Forces.

"No. We can't have Elvis pull any favors. The country doesn't look favorably on boys who shirk their duty to the military. It'd be bad business in the long run.

"Elvis, you have records that haven't been released and a movie in the can. We can stretch out the product we have. There'll be a certain dark period, but that will only double the demand for your records and movies once you get out of the service."

Parker made arrangements to make the situation as pleasant as possible. The army allowed Elvis to live off base during boot camp in a rented house as long as he showed up for reveille on time. That news cheered Elvis up considerably, and he immediately decided his parents, Red, and Earl would stay with him during his basic training in Texas.

And just like that, Gladys's baby was off to the army.

On the morning he was inducted, Elvis spent his last hours as a civilian sequestered in his room, doubled over with anxiety and shaking with the fear of change. He snapped at anyone who asked him a question, and found fault with everything—his breakfast was too cold, his shoes were dirty, his clothes hadn't been properly ironed. Nothing was right with his world anymore.

Carrying his suitcase, he walked down the stairs with the step of a condemned man. No matter how much Parker tried to reassure him, Elvis had a premonition that life as he knew it was over forever; the good times would be little more than memories. And in fact he was right, but in a way he never anticipated.

Less than two weeks after Elvis was transferred to Fort Hood for his basic training, his base of operations had moved from Graceland to an isolated house Vernon had found in the dusty burg of Killeen, Texas. Elvis warned everyone against making fun of his shorn head. Vanity aside, foremost on his mind was how he would survive two months in Killeen—a hot, humid, hellhole in the middle of nowhere, with bugs the size of small poodles. If the bugs didn't get him, the surging mob of fans surrounding the house would. It must have taken the locals all of an hour to find out where Elvis was staying.

Elvis had never been one to work out regularly, so the first weeks of training left him sore and walking like an old man. He'd come home aching and dog tired. He'd eat dinner in sullen silence, then trudge off to bed, already dreading the alarm clock that rang in pitch blackness. Elvis hated the army, his career seemed like a misty memory, and he was depressed by his surroundings: the steamy weather made breathing difficult, and your clothes were perpetually sticky and damp; moist sheets were scented with mildew; bugs covered grocery items and burrowed inside the packaging as well.

Elvis couldn't let go of what he'd left behind. His body might be in Texas, but the rest of his being was still firmly planted in Memphis. On most mornings when he woke up, his mind took him to Beale Street, and he imagined listening to the musicians playing their final set before he headed for an early-morning burger at his favorite all-night diner. After dinner, when boredom threatened to drive him stir crazy, Elvis pined over his inability to go out to the Rainbow Roller Rink for a night of fun or to sit in a huge movie theater with some friends. Lying in bed trying to sleep, he tried to blank out images of Anita in the arms of another man. Suddenly he was feeling very possessive of her and wishing their relationship was exclusive. More than anything, he missed performing and feeling the warmth of the audience wash over him. His life source was slowly leaking out, and his hands were tied to refill it.

Elvis knew how much could change in two years. It was time enough for a new performer to take the country by storm and steal away his fans, time enough for Hollywood to find a new leading man, time enough to become yesterday's star. He was sure his career was as good as dead.

Elvis wallowed emotionally in his predicament and, in his deepest depression, even took this turn of events as proof of his unworthiness to have lived instead of Jesse. Jesse wouldn't have brought the family so far only to lose it this way. Bad things like this happened only because he deserved it. This emotional non sequitur—taking the blame for situations out of his control because he felt so unworthy and lacking—would prove Elvis's ultimate downfall when faced with the ultimate crisis.

The water in the Fort Hood area smelled brackish and looked tainted, as if something was fermenting in the pipes that carried it. It was so bad that Elvis ordered bottled water, but it was too late to prevent Earl and Gladys from getting sick. Earl, who was now working as Elvis's publicist, recovered, but Gladys could hardly drag herself from the bedroom to the kitchen for a morning cup of coffee before heading straight back to bed. Despite the stifling August heat, chills racked her body; but more alarming was her deathly, yellow-tinged skin color.

Gladys was frightened, especially being so far away from home. After a family meeting, it was decided that Earl and Vernon would take Gladys back to Memphis to see a trusted physician and to recuperate in the homier surroundings of Graceland.

Elvis convinced himself it was heat exhaustion, and while concerned, he wasn't worried. In truth, he was secretly relieved Gladys was going home. With her gone, he could invite in some of the pretty young girls hanging around outside his door. But Vernon feared something was very wrong with Gladys, even though he kept his thoughts to himself and presented a calm and reassuring front.

Gladys was getting worse with each passing day and spent the entire trip home on her back, whimpering and feverish. Vernon was completely attentive, holding her hand, keeping her cool with damp towels on her forehead, and comforting her with quiet humor and strong arms.

Finally back in Memphis, they headed straight to the doctor, who diagnosed Gladys with hepatitis. He prescribed some medicine and promised it would make her a new woman. To make sure she got complete bed rest, he wanted to keep her in the hospital for a few days.

When Earl called Elvis, he could hear the sounds of a party—Red had brought some girls over. Elvis was surprised Gladys was genuinely ill but relieved she was on the road to recovery. With his mother gone, Elvis was free to do as he pleased. He raced home every night from training, ate a quick meal, and was ready for an evening of fun. Out of all the girls he had ever met, he found the local girls among the most willing to please, and he silently prayed that Gladys not return to Texas at all.

Back in Memphis, doctors puzzled over why Gladys wasn't responding to the medication. They tried several different combinations, only to see her condition worsen. Her body was weak; she was overweight and had terrible muscle tone, a weak heart, and a bloated liver from years of alcohol abuse. More than that, Gladys lacked the spark vital for recovery. Vernon had to lift her up just so she could sip from a glass. Her soul appeared as weak and tired as her body and ready to take its leave.

The doctor didn't tell Vernon anything he hadn't already sensed. A decision was quickly made to send for Elvis in hopes of boosting Gladys's spirits and reviving her will and fight. Within a few hours, Elvis had been granted an emergency leave of absence and was on a plane for Memphis.

When he arrived at the hospital, Elvis was as white as a sheet and too stunned to say much of anything. Tears welled in his eyes when he saw Gladys—she was a wisp of her former self. He sat on the bed and held her. Her voice was weak when she spoke, but she was obviously happy to see her son. So it was strange when she insisted he go home to Graceland and sleep there instead of staying with her. When Gladys said goodbye to Elvis, her eyes filled with intense emotion and premonition, staring at Elvis as if she knew she'd never see him again.

That night, Elvis decided to go to a movie, insisting Anita, Red, and Earl accompany him. He was hoping it would be a diversion, but he couldn't stop fidgeting, thinking about his mother. After the movie, they stopped for cheeseburgers then headed back to Graceland.

Around three in the morning, Vernon called to tell Elvis that Gladys had died. She was only 43. Elvis was, in a word, destroyed. For days, he would ask numbly, "What am I gonna do? How am I gonna live without her? I killed her. I killed my mama."

Time dragged. Elvis's grief came in waves, and when it hit, he'd sag against the wall or sink to the floor, weeping agonized tears. His relief at seeing her leave Texas now paralyzed him with guilt. He hated women for their hold over his loins that made him betray Gladys and wish her gone. Elvis also harbored incredible anger at Gladys for not letting him stay at the hospital and for leaving him alone in this world. She'd left him and gone to Jesse, who Elvis had always believed was her preferred son. Too distraught to turn his brain off, Elvis saw a doctor who prescribed him some sleeping pills.

The next 48 hours were a blur for Elvis. When he wasn't weeping, Elvis walked around like a zombie, his stupor interrupted by occasional flashes of temper. The day of the funeral was the worst of Elvis's life. It started out badly the moment the attendants came to transport Gladys's body back to the Memphis funeral home. As they wheeled the casket through the front door, Elvis broke free from Vernon's grasp and ran after it. He threw himself on top of the casket, crying hysterically.

The parlor men made the mistake of trying to pry him loose. *"Don't touch her!"* Elvis screamed. When they made another move toward him, he started flailing at them, impotent punches landing only on air. Earl shouted at the attendants to stop and motioned for them to just wait until Elvis was ready to let go. When he had finally worn himself out, Vernon stepped forward and gently led Elvis away.

He sat through the service with his head bowed, avoiding the eyes of the other mourners, unwilling to share his grief. The ride to the cemetery was strained but calm. Elvis managed to keep his composure until it was time for the attendants to lower Gladys's casket into the grave. His body twitched, but Vernon grabbed his arm to keep him from making a lunge at the casket. Elvis was beside himself with panic and grief, babbling incoherently just loud enough to be heard by those around him.

He talked to Gladys all the way into the ground until Vernon and Miss Minnie gently led him away. Elvis was so emotionally drained that they had to half carry him to the car. It was a relief to everyone when Elvis passed out, and Vernon left him there in the driveway for over an hour before waking him.

Elvis left Graceland early the next day for Texas, his leave officially over with the funeral. He was ready to go before anyone else was awake, eager to get back to boot camp, finding it preferable to the ghosts at Graceland. The doctor who had prescribed the sleeping pills had okayed a refill in case Elvis had trouble sleeping. He tossed the bottle into his bag, with no one giving it a second thought.

They set off in a car caravan, Elvis again accompanied by Earl, Vernon, Red, and Miss Minnie. Greenwood remembered seeing the change in him. "The Elvis we had all known was gone forever; he'd been buried with Gladys."

From that point on, Elvis was on a collision course with tragedy. It took 20 years, but the roller coaster ride had passed its highest point and was about to begin its long, slow, final descent. The change was apparent almost immediately.

Anita came down to Texas a few weeks after the funeral but didn't stay long. Elvis didn't go to the door to see her off, so she walked over to him. "I shouldn't say anything at all to you, because you don't listen, but maybe it'll get through anyway. You got to stop blaming the world for everything bad that happens to you. Just because you're hurting and angry doesn't give you the right to be hurtful. I'm not saying it's deliberate. Sometimes, without knowing it, people hurt first to keep from being hurt themselves. That's a good way to end up alone."

No matter how much Elvis complained at home about the service, he was a model soldier. With Gladys gone, it suddenly became very important for him to make friends. Instead of being alone with his grief, he sought to diffuse it through distraction. Once a week he invited a handful of soldiers over for a home-cooked meal and their choice of expensive liquors.

During this time, Elvis became obsessed with making sure no woman he slept with was a mother, and he felt more secure with the teenage girls. He also found it difficult to sleep by himself anymore. He needed a body next to his—it didn't really matter whose. If therapy had been as socially acceptable then as it is now, Elvis might have been able to understand his sudden obsessions and work to resolve them.

In late September 1958 Elvis boarded a train for New York and then shipped out to West Germany on the USS *Randall*. He watched the coastline shrink, thinking nothing would ever be right for him. He knew he'd never be whole again and was resigned to play out the hand that life had dealt him.

Elvis arrived in Germany with his aching spirit resigned to his fate but was quickly and pleasantly surprised to discover that his fame had preceded him. The German people were more respectful and less intrusive than the American fans, and Elvis basked in the warmth of their approval without being blinded by the glare of his celebrity. Some of the less intimidated soldiers sought out his company, and he cultivated a cocoon that kept him from being alone, even if it didn't ward off his emptiness. Army life was undemanding and left him with ample free time to sample the German culture, especially the *fräulein*. His first girlfriend was a buxom blonde named Magrite, but she was soon replaced by an even younger American beauty who became his hope for salvation.

The first thing that struck Elvis about Priscilla Beaulieu was her "eerie familiarity." It took him several minutes before he put a finger on it—she looked uncannily like faded photos he'd seen of Gladys as a young girl. She knew who Elvis was but wasn't in awe of him or his celebrity. Being the daughter of an air force captain, Priscilla had traveled extensively; as a result, she exuded a maturity that belied her 14 years. Her subtle reserve intrigued Elvis; she wasn't like any other young girl he'd ever met.

Priscilla's age presented a few problems in Germany. While fans were respectful as far as keeping a polite distance, the press covered his every move. Elvis found privacy more difficult to obtain in Germany than in Memphis, where he could retreat behind the gates of Graceland. He once took Priscilla to a movie, and when they came out, a crowd of almost 100 people stood quietly across the street, just to catch a glimpse of him.

A few of the local papers found out Priscilla's age and made subtle but pointed references to her youth. Elvis immediately worried that the negative tone would turn people against him. He tried to diffuse any potential gossip by going underground with their relationship, which had barely gotten past the hand-holding stage. They spent time together in out-of-the-way restaurants or in parks out in the countryside. Elvis had never been on a real picnic before, with a blanket and a basket full of food, and the magic of the experience left him starry-eyed. He was living in a fantasy world, moving through a time and place that couldn't last.

Because they met toward the end of his enlistment, Elvis knew their time together was limited, and that made each moment particularly precious. But what made Priscilla more of an obsession was the growing notion that she was more than the spitting image of a young Gladys. Everything about Priscilla convinced him that she actually embodied the spirit of his dead mother.

Unlike the girls he met in bars or picked out of the crowd at performances or from the throngs in front of Graceland, Priscilla didn't throw herself at Elvis, and her bearing commanded respect. She was well schooled but unpretentious, with an unassuming but warm, sparkling personality. Somehow, Jesse had answered his prayers and sent Gladys back to him in the person of Priscilla. He didn't pretend to understand how miracles worked, he only believed in their possibility. He was being given a second chance to prove himself. He immediately put Priscilla on a pedestal alongside the gilded image of his deceased mother, whose memory shone more brightly in his thoughts as each day passed. In return, all that he expected back was a sense of wholeness and perfect, unconditional love.

The illusion that Gladys lived on through Priscilla was at once erotically arousing, emotionally satisfying, and a fountainhead of guilt. Long-buried Oedipal desires scratched at the surface of his consciousness. Their presence caused Elvis enough anxiety to keep him from trying to break down Priscilla's defenses so he could sleep with her. She was too good, simple, and pure for that, and even *thoughts* of her flesh under his made Elvis shrink with shame. Theirs was a relationship that would transcend the dirty physical.

Elvis was so wrapped up in his own reverie that he was blind to events happening under his own nose. Vernon and Miss Minnie had joined Elvis a few weeks after he arrived in Germany as a support network. Vernon loved exploring new places and made friends easily with his good-old-boy demeanor. Among his best new pals were an army sergeant and his wife, who were originally from Alabama. They spent many a fun-filled evening out at local *nausbiers* enjoying beers between oompah-pahs.

Elvis portrayed his father as the grieving widower, which is what he thought he ought to be, and spoke sincerely about their loss. For however much Vernon missed Gladys, and they had been together more than 20 years, his loss was minimal compared to Elvis's. Since the day her twin son died, Gladys had never been Vernon's emotional strength. They were financial partners for good and for bad, occasionally found physical release in each other's arms, and shared in the day-to-day struggles, but they had not been emotional partners. They didn't even really share in the raising of their only child. Elvis had firmly been her domain, with Vernon relegated to the position of interested spectator. If anything, Gladys's death opened up a new world for Vernon—a chance to find someone who paid attention to *him,* who noticed whether or not he was there, and cared. Vernon missed Gladys's presence because it was so familiar, but his heart had not gone into seclusion.

When the army sergeant got involved with a project that required longer hours, Vernon gladly helped him out by escorting his wife, Dee, to dinner so she wouldn't have to be home alone waiting. Suddenly, Vernon found himself sad when Dee said goodnight and shut the door. What he didn't realize was that Dee felt the same emotion as she watched him walk away in the darkness.

After a particularly romantic evening, Vernon blurted out his feelings and was overwhelmed when Dee admitted she loved him, too. They conducted their romance with the utmost discretion and managed to keep it secret for several months before an American reporter happened upon them at a remote village restaurant and recognized the handsome older man as Elvis Presley's father. Earl managed to keep it out of the papers for the time being, but it was only a matter of time because Dee had left her husband and planned to file for divorce. Despite his anxiety over Elvis eventually finding out, Vernon was not overly concerned about the publicity, because he was very much in love.

Elvis was too wrapped up in Priscilla to notice his father's happiness. Even though his tour of duty was almost over and he'd soon be returning to Memphis, he was confident he and Priscilla had a future. His last week in Germany was filled with emotion and promise, but he left with the full assurance that he and Priscilla were being guided from above and their reunion was a *fait accompli*.

Elvis was officially discharged on May 5, 1960, but Vernon flew back to Memphis with Dee a couple days earlier. On his way out the door to the airport, Vernon told Elvis about Dee and their intention to marry. He was relieved at Elvis's apparent calm acceptance of the news, but it was wishful thinking. Elvis had just been so shocked he had blanked out. As the news sank in, Elvis threw a tantrum of frightening proportions that brought his neighbors running outside. He hurled furniture at the walls and left holes in the walls with his fists. Vernon had betrayed Gladys and had betrayed him. The tentative bridge of trust they had been developing crumbled like dust in the shockwaves that followed Vernon's announcement. Elvis knew in his heart he could never forgive Vernon if he went through with his plan to marry.

Dee was a striking woman, blonde and about 20 years younger than Vernon, but it was obvious that she loved him dearly. They fit together well, and everyone at Graceland couldn't help but be happy for them—Miss Minnie especially. But the joyous atmosphere was about to be tempered with Elvis's arrival home. A party had been planned to celebrate Elvis's return, and to no one's surprise, Vernon and Dee opted not to attend. Instead, Vernon took her for a night out at some of Memphis's finer clubs, excited to show her around her new home.

Red picked up Elvis from the airport, and when he stepped out of the car at Graceland, Elvis stood just taking in the surroundings. He took deep breaths, filling his lungs with the familiar scents of his home. He reacquainted himself by walking through every room. Except for the removal of Gladys's clothes and other personal belongings, nothing had changed in two years.

"Elvis was pleased we had a party planned, but it wasn't a good sign of things to come when Elvis didn't ask after Vernon not being there," Earl recalled. "When Elvis cut the cake Miss Minnie had baked, he nearly chopped his tie in two, and as we all laughed, it appeared the old Elvis was finally back. But once the guests left, his mood turned dark, as if another person had suddenly appeared." "Is Daddy with that whore of his?" he demanded of Earl. "You know she's only with him because of *my* money … nothing more than a gold-digger."

Elvis began pacing with agitation and pulled a small vial of pills out of his pocket. He grabbed a nearby bottle of beer and washed two pills down. When he saw Earl's concern, he bristled. "These are to help me relax so I can get to sleep. Doctor in Germany said it helps get over jet lag. I know what I'm doing," he added with an edge.

His first week back was hectic. Parker arrived to brief Elvis on the status of his career, and Elvis was shocked to see it so healthy—record sales were still strong, RCA had the next batch of songs for him to record ready to go, Vegas wanted him for some dates, and his next movie was a go. Elvis seemed dazed that his public hadn't forgotten him after all and grateful to Parker for his part.

But for all his relief that he had survived a two-year layoff, Elvis expressed mild chagrin that he had no say in the songs he'd be recording or the movie he'd be starring in. Parker ignored the complaint and forged ahead with a complex accounting of other business transactions that left Elvis with a headache.

Once alone, Elvis roamed the house restlessly. Everywhere he turned there were still reminders of Gladys: her favorite chair, her bedroom and the pillow she slept on, and the empty remains of a chicken coop in the backyard beside a garden plot now overgrown with weeds. He still missed hearing her voice and seeing her sweet face. Nothing and nobody could ever completely fill the void, which made Priscilla's importance that much greater—especially now because he had as good as buried Vernon, too.

Reverting to his old form, Elvis turned to sex to ease his pain. It was a predictable pattern: Red would go find a willing girl—preferably two—bring them back, and then discretely leave. One night during that first week, Elvis was thumbing through the script of the film he was set to do, G./. *Blues*. He threw it down in disgust, amazed at how quickly the studio was able to take advantage of any situation. "I ain't out of the army a week and they wanna put me right back in," he sighed.

That night, he orchestrated an orgy with himself, Earl, and four girls, none of them over 17. Midway through, he got the idea to make a home movie of the occasion and had Earl set up the lights and camera, and he shot until the film ran out. Several more times that week, the orgy was repeated, each one filmed. The faces changed and each group got younger, until on the final evening there were four 14-year-olds—with the bodies of women a decade older. Somehow, Elvis managed to get the film discretely developed and planned a night at the movies with Red and a couple of his army buddies, who had been given jobs as gofers.

The movies were Elvis's latest pride and joy. He and his boys watched parts of them every day until he left for Miami to appear at the Fontainebleau Hotel with Frank Sinatra. Before heading to the airport, he stashed the films in a drawer without giving them a second thought.

Chapter 12

A NEW WOMAN
OF THE HOUSE

Sinatra treated Elvis politely but carried himself with the bearing of a man who knows his position. Elvis was courteous and intimidated, but on stage he felt Sinatra's equal. The concert went well and Elvis left soon after, curious about Sinatra's special interest in his upcoming film.

G.I. Blues was a mindless star vehicle memorable only for his costar, the stunning Juliet Prowse. As he had done before, he went after a lady of class to prove himself worthy and equal, believing it would gain him acceptance in Hollywood. Their affair was heated, and Juliet lavished attention on Elvis, although she preferred to spend nights at home rather than out on the town. Elvis naturally shied away from parties or gatherings where he might feel out of place or awkward, so he was more than happy to acquiesce.

Elvis returned to Graceland after the movie wrapped, and Juliet kept in constant touch. Nobody could understand why she always used a code name when she called, and Elvis just shrugged when asked and gave a half smile. At a rehearsal shortly before he was to leave for Vegas, he finally admitted what was going on. Elvis wasn't Juliet's only beau of the moment—she was also the apple of another singer's blue eyes. Elvis felt supremely smug and superior, sweeping Sinatra's lady off her feet.

In the middle of his story, a phone rang. "Oh, oh, Elvis, it's probably Frank," someone wisecracked. In the days after that, if there was a knock on the door or an unexpected phone call, "Oh oh, it's probably Frank" became the running joke. Elvis laughed harder than anyone, tickled at having put one over on the Chairman of the Board.

Elvis and Juliet hooked up back in Vegas for a couple of days before she headed to Los Angeles for some business commitments. One evening Elvis was in his dressing room, cooling down after a performance, when a stagehand peeked in and told him Frank Sinatra was outside to see him. Elvis laughed, assuming one of the guys had put him up to it.

He looked up into his mirror in time to see Frank Sinatra walk through the dressing room door, accompanied by two unpleasant-looking companions. The conversation was extremely civil and very brief. Sinatra complimented him on his show and on the completion of his new film, and offered him some free advice: if Elvis wanted to continue working in good health, he should make sure he wasn't stepping on the wrong toes. Without ever mentioning her name or losing his smile, Sinatra succeeded in making Juliet Prowse the biggest turn-off Elvis could imagine.

From that night on, Elvis completely broke off all contact with her. Prowse attempted to reach him for several weeks and then abruptly stopped—to his immense relief.

FEELING EMPTY

As soon as Dee's divorce was final, she and Vernon got married in Alabama, partly to get away from the Memphis press and partly because they both had relatives there. Elvis refused to go, saying he was too busy with work. He also forbade anyone else to go, except for Miss Minnie.

To Vernon's and Dee's faces, he was merely rude and uncommunicative—a spoiled child punishing those around him because he didn't get his way. Vernon would have been shocked had he known the full measure of disrespect Elvis harbored. One night, everyone had just sat down to eat when Vernon and Dee stopped in to say goodbye on their way out. Elvis waited until Miss Minnie walked out of the room and then suddenly bolted to his feet and walked around the table, picking up plate after plate and smashing each one into the wall. The room was covered with food, and everyone stayed stock still, not wanting to inflame him even more.

"Goddam them to hell," he yelled as the plates were flying. "How *dare* he bring that bitch into Mama's house? It makes me sick. If it wasn't outta respect for Mama, I'd throw 'em both out on the street and tell 'em to go get jobs."

Elvis might have felt better had he let off steam directly by having it out with Vernon man to man, but he didn't dare confront him. Gladys had always let him know in no uncertain terms that disrespect toward his father upset her and wouldn't be tolerated. Kin was kin.

Elvis was full of paradoxes that pulled him in opposite directions. Despite his acute disapproval, once Vernon married Dee, she became extended family whether Elvis liked it or not.

Beyond that, Elvis never had the confidence or nerve to stand up to his father. He could only rant and rave behind his back and cut him out emotionally. He also bad-mouthed Dee any chance he got, despite everyone else thinking she was one of the sweetest people they'd ever met.

Having eyes and ears everywhere, Parker was well aware of the rift that had opened between Vernon and Elvis. The Colonel liked Vernon and considered him an important ally. He doubted Elvis would make a stand against Vernon, but he never took chances. During their next meeting, Parker impassively counseled Elvis against the dangers of a family feud leaking out to the public and even joked that it wouldn't look very good in the papers if the father of the country's most popular singer went back to living in a shack in Mississippi.

Elvis bristled inside, but at that same moment he had other aggravations on his mind that were bothering him more. Parker had brought over another script for a movie that Hollywood wanted Elvis to do, and he also had with him a recording schedule for some new songs for the record label. Elvis had been unhappy with several selections RCA had chosen for him, and many of the new songs bothered him even more. He didn't mind doing some of what RCA wanted; he just wanted the chance to pick a couple out himself. He had complained to Parker before without result and brought it up again.

"I thought we agreed I'd get to do some other things?"

"You don't tamper with success," Parker told him. "Maybe later."

"It's always later. I don' see why I have to keep waiting. They're making enough money off me, the least they can do is let me sing a couple of songs that make me feel good."

"Stop being difficult, Elvis. I'll see what I can do, but there's no reason to run off half-cocked."

After Parker left, Elvis remarked bitterly, "Sometimes I think Parker forgets he works for me. I'm tired of fighting the people who are *supposed* to be on my side."

Graceland was like Grand Central Station in the hectic months following Elvis's return. When Gladys was alive, it had been her house, and Elvis didn't let his buddies hang out there much. Now, in addition to Earl, Vernon, Dee, and Miss Minnie, several of his entourage were living there as well. He was still haunted by the specter of Gladys, which in turn made him dwell on her alter ego, Priscilla, ever more often.

As Elvis reminisced, fantasized, and romanticized their time together, Priscilla grew to a larger-than-life idol in his mind. She was young, untainted, and moldable. He turned her into the perfect girl he imagined she could be, leaving no room for who she really was. He began to yearn for her terribly. He wrote her long missives and checked the mail every day for her replies. If he was out of town, he had the letters forwarded—all the while maintaining his carefree bachelor ways. He still pushed sexual feelings about Priscilla off to the side, keeping his guilt at bay.

Elvis's loneliness and depression overwhelmed him anytime he wasn't actively distracted by sex, work, or the constant attention of his group of followers. At night, he was restless and itching to be on the move, but going out in public meant dealing with fans. For as much as he loved them, he'd get weary of being smothered. Therefore, he would either isolate himself at home or rent out a place and isolate himself there.

Fewer and fewer things gave Elvis pleasure anymore. For someone who'd grown up so poor, rather than appreciate the finer things he now had in life, he seemed angry because the material things weren't enough. They hadn't given him the sense of wholeness he expected, so he occasionally treated his things with disdain. In his room, expensive pieces of jewelry were flung all over, some of it twisted from being stepped on.

In the fall of 1960, after he'd returned from yet another movie in Hollywood, Elvis was particularly irritable and moody. It was like living with two different people, or identical twins with opposite personalities. Elvis could still be extremely charming when he wanted to be—he just didn't want to make the effort that much anymore. The exception to that was with children. With them he was always good, kind, and considerate, no matter what else was going on in his life.

Over the years stacks and stacks of letters poured in from families saying their child was sick or dying and that the child's greatest wish was to talk to Elvis. Or the letters might say how a phone call from him would help a child battle back from this disease or that injury. It was heartbreaking, and having that kind of responsibility heaped on his shoulders put a lot of pressure on Elvis.

A couple of secretaries worked out of a spare room in Graceland, going through the mail, and Earl developed a special system for letters concerning sick children. A questionnaire was sent to the parents with a return envelope, marked with a red line down the side. Those envelopes were the first to be opened on any given day. The questionnaire asked for the doctor's name and phone number, the nature of the illness, and other pertinent information to make sure the letter wasn't a fraud. Only about a fourth of the questionnaires were returned.

Obviously, the situation had to be serious, or else Elvis would have spent all his days on the phone. Of those that checked out, if the child was still in the hospital—often he or she had recovered by the time all the paperwork was done—Elvis would put in a phone call. Elvis enjoyed making the time and was thrilled to hear the little voices on the other end light up. Several times, Elvis did more than just call. If he found out the parents weren't able to continue treatment because of money problems, or that other kids in the family were going without because of the medical bills, Elvis had Earl make arrangements to pick up the medical bills until the child recovered. The only stipulation was that it was to be kept a secret. It was a reminder of his basic good soul, no matter how he behaved in other situations.

The contrast between the public image of Elvis as a happy, carefree man on top of the world who had everything going his way and the moody, depressed man he could be at home was carefully orchestrated by Parker. In public, whether in Memphis, Hollywood, or Vegas, at concerts or out among his fans, Elvis became the Elvis the public wanted to see.

The publicity machinery surrounding Elvis helped maintain a certain public image in a lot of little ways. For example, if a celebrity or a politician was visiting Memphis, a greeting, in Elvis's name, was sent to the individual along with an invitation to Graceland if he was in town. Like many celebrities, Elvis had a public persona that was created and maintained by others over the course of his career. And as the years went by, the public image of Elvis grew further and further removed from the man he became.

It was obvious Elvis was lonely. Ironically, his countless one-night stands and brief affairs only left him more and more despondent, cynical, and resentful. No woman he met—whether starlet, famous actress, or hometown girl—met his impossible expectations and qualifications. As soon as she exerted any spark of independence or showed any sign of intellectual or professional equality, she was dropped. Elvis wasn't secure enough in himself not to feel threatened by a true equal, which was another reason he gravitated toward young girls.

With each failure, Priscilla's star grew ever brighter. And as the end of the year approached, he began to dwell on Priscilla, bringing her up out of the blue in conversation and speaking of her as if she were a fairy-tale princess. The girl he described *was* too good to be true, and his wishful, insistent fantasy doomed their relationship before it began. Time and distance had molded Priscilla into the perfect woman, and he found himself pining for her.

Elvis hit a real low point a couple of weeks before Christmas, as shiny decorations lined Memphis streets and a holiday atmosphere brightened the city. All the festive cheer made Elvis miserable and grumpy about everything. He was particularly agitated at not having any control over his music or movies, and his anger festered inside him like a cancer.

"I'm getting fed up with Parker refusing to take me seriously on this," he vented. "I appreciate all he's done, but it's *my* career, not his."

He resolved to have it out with Parker and called to arrange a meeting. Once Elvis jumped on something, he couldn't rest until he had seen it through, plus he wanted to act while he was angry and felt sure enough about it. Confronting Parker was scary, but he challenged himself to take control. Maybe he could rid himself of that ever-present shaky feeling if he stopped letting other people have the last word.

Parker showed up, his face impassive as always, and they went into the music room and shut the door. Their conversation didn't last very long, and when they came out, Elvis's face was pasty and his eyes curiously flat—the look of a condemned man. Elvis had underestimated Parker and his ability to keep his piece of the Presley pie firmly in hand. It wasn't until years later that Elvis revealed to Earl what had transpired between them, and by then it was too late to undo the damage.

That night he told Earl about a book he was reading on reincarnation and wondered who he had been in his past lives. His otherworldly thoughts brought Gladys and Jesse to mind, and he remembered conversations he'd had with them.

"They come a lot at night in my sleep. When my time comes to join them. I wonder how it'll feel to look at Jesse and see myself. I can't see them in the day, but I can hear them. And I can *feel* them when I'm talking to them. It gives me so much comfort to know they're here with me. They say I won't have to wait long before I join them."

Elvis seemed unafraid of death. "When it's my time, I have a feeling I'll be more than ready to go. I'll be sad at leaving certain people behind, but happy at who I'll be going to meet."

His problem was how to get through this life, and he came to the conclusion that the only person capable of making him happy was Priscilla. In that instant, he decided she had to come to Graceland—*now*—to celebrate Christmas.

"'Scilla is my destiny—and I'm hers."

Priscilla's arrival had Graceland abuzz with activity, and on the surface it appeared Elvis was coming back from his long battle against his grief over Gladys's death. Had anybody dared to peek under the comforting outer layer of his impulsiveness to bring Priscilla to Graceland, a darker truth would have reared its ugly head. Desperate to find a cure for the racking lack of control he felt over his life, which had been exacerbated by the recent confrontation with Parker, Elvis viewed Priscilla as a solution.

He was losing his balance over the abyss beneath him, and he counted on her not to let him slip off. Priscilla did her best but found it impossible to save Elvis from himself.

During the weeks of Priscilla's holiday visit, life at Graceland took a turn for the normal. Elvis lavished time and attention on Priscilla, and didn't so much as look in another girl's direction. He went to bed at a decent hour and was the first one up and ready to start the day. He refrained from inviting over the regular assortment of hangers-on and kept the number of people at Graceland down to a minimum in order to devote his full attention to her. He even found it in his heart to be more polite and less vicious toward Dee. It was like being with Scrooge on Christmas Day, and everyone basked in the light of Elvis's happiness.

Priscilla endured the scrutiny of everyone with admirable grace. She was described as sweet, very pretty, very sexy, young, and *very* naïve—but not simple in the way of Gladys. She had the innocent and idealistic outlook of a well-cared-for teenager. Elvis presented her as a princess, and she happily accepted the role, not knowing what a straitjacket it would become.

Elvis thought she was perfect. "'Scilla makes me feel like singing all the time. I don't know what it is about her."

She was one of the few things Vernon and Elvis saw eye to eye on. Vernon made a constant fuss over Priscilla—"Wouldn' mama jus' love her?"—and between the two of them, her head was spinning.

For her part, Priscilla seemed just as delighted to be back in America as she was to be at Graceland with Elvis. She bought magazines and wanted to catch up on the latest trends and fashions, go to the movies, watch television, and go out and have real American shakes and burgers. Her enthusiasm was contagious, and the house radiated a life that had been missing for years.

Later it would become painfully clear that those closest to Elvis—and especially Elvis himself—put too much on Priscilla's shoulders; the expectations of what she could do were too high. She was on a pedestal so high up that she would soon be gasping for breath at the elevated altitude.

As the end of Priscilla's holiday vacation neared, the thought of her leaving drove Elvis to despair. The solution was simple—she simply had to stay. She could go to school in Memphis and live at Graceland full time. Vernon was in full support. After weeks of peaceful cohabitation, Vernon was apprehensive of the mood Elvis would revert to if Priscilla left. Like everyone else, he believed Priscilla's mere presence would solve everything and make Graceland a home, happily ever after.

With Vernon on the upstairs extension, Elvis talked to Joe Beaulieu for close to an hour, while Priscilla sat listening quietly but anxiously. The rest of the household paced nervously, waiting for an answer. After a sometimes-impassioned conversation, it had been miraculously arranged. Priscilla would move to Graceland as a guest of Vernon and Dee's, who would take personal responsibility for chaperoning her. Elvis picked up Priscilla and swung her in a joyous circle. The king had claimed his queen.

Unfortunately, the honeymoon period was short-lived.

During the holidays, Elvis had focused exclusively on Priscilla, a luxury afforded by a hiatus from career commitments and by the fact that he didn't yet possess her. Once her residency at Graceland was ensured and Priscilla was under his control, he turned his attention elsewhere. Almost immediately, Elvis took Priscilla's presence for granted. And since he didn't and couldn't make love to her, he was now ready and needy for the next conquest.

Elvis enrolled Priscilla in an all-girls school, Immaculate Conception, wanting her well educated and sheltered from the attention of teenage boys. Under the guise of complying with Mr. Beaulieu's conditions, Elvis tightened a protective net around Priscilla that effectively made her a prisoner. In the beginning, Elvis personally dropped her off in the morning and picked her up at night whenever he was in town or not in the recording studio. He surprised her with lavish gifts and treated her with kind words and actions.

The only one not thrilled with Priscilla was Parker. While it might be less difficult to pass her off as a friend of the family here for a visit, convincing the country that Elvis was the platonic host of a live-in 15-year-old girl would be almost impossible. The only saving grace was the number of people who lived at Graceland and the fact that Elvis kept her under close wraps and didn't flaunt her in public.

While she adjusted to her new home, Priscilla seemed content to spend time at Graceland, but as she acclimated to her surroundings, the natural restlessness of a teenager surfaced. Elvis sternly cautioned her against going out alone at any time, citing his concern for her safety.

Starting in 1961, Parker steered Elvis away from touring as a singer and more toward being a Hollywood movie star, where one could make the most money in the shortest amount of time and with the least effort. His albums sold the same, regardless of whether he promoted them on the road, so he confined regular live performing to Las Vegas. As a result, Elvis spent a lot of time away from Memphis in California and Nevada. This was a catch Priscilla hadn't contemplated, and the realization they'd be apart upset her. When she first pouted about an upcoming separation,

Elvis cuddled her and comforted her, promising she would come with him during the summer. He told her they'd be together all the time after she graduated, and he was so sincere she melted and obediently dried her tears with brave resolve. What he neglected to mention was that he preferred her confined at Graceland. He assumed it prevented her from meeting any young men, and it allowed him the freedom to have affairs.

When he came back from a trip, he would dote on her for a day or two before getting distracted with a rehearsal or an evening with his boys. But even when summer came, conveniently for Elvis, his schedule rarely permitted Priscilla to travel with him, so they were apart quite often. A beautiful bird in a gilded cage, Priscilla was just as much a prisoner of his success and emotional shortcomings as he was.

Every time Elvis went to Hollywood to make a picture, the newspapers would link him to some actress or starlet. And for the most part the stories were true. He didn't care if the women of the moment knew about each other, but he did not want Priscilla to know. He cancelled his subscription to the newspaper and *Variety*, but Priscilla doggedly scoured the school library to read the gossip. Word of his romances made Priscilla more petu-lant before each trip, creating an uncomfortable tension between them. Elvis denied the stories to Priscilla and passed them off as Hollywood gossip.

As with Gladys, Elvis called home every day, but in this case, it was mostly to make sure Priscilla was home. He'd laugh off her concern and patiently explain the ways of Hollywood. She was young and in love enough to accept what he said, because she desperately *wanted* to believe he wouldn't lie to her. Everyone at Graceland was under explicit orders to avoid talking to Priscilla as much as possible. It was very clear that if any-one let on about anything, he or she would be out the door immediately.

Elvis was able to keep the peace with his convincing explanations for a long time. But as Priscilla got older and wiser, she also got less trusting. It began taking much more effort on Elvis's part to smooth over the bumps. Eventually his lies would catch up with him.

Chapter 13

WALKING A FINE LINE

When Elvis was younger, sex was a harmless sowing of oats, good-natured fun, and experimentation. Now his exploits carried so much baggage, hidden meanings, and power struggles that sex was harmful not just to him but to every woman he became intimate with, whether physically or emotionally—especially the girl he professed to love.

For all their problems, Vernon had never cheated on Gladys, but that respect for fidelity had not passed on to his son. Had Elvis been able to establish a fulfilling sexual relationship with Priscilla, he might have been less inclined to seek the flesh of others. He was greatly aroused by her and admitted they played "games" but stopped short of consummation. Instead, he'd tuck her in, have one of his entourage procure a hasty date, and have it off in the back seat of the limo—half the time without leaving the driveway.

These raw encounters highlighted the pureness of his relationship with Priscilla. He couldn't begin to understand the real reason he felt so guilty about wanting to sleep with her, so he explained his determination to hold off on their physical relationship until a proper time by saying that with Priscilla, it was sacred.

While Priscilla pined alone at Graceland, Elvis amused himself with the girls he had on call in Hollywood, Las Vegas, and Palm Springs. Not all these encounters went smoothly, and Elvis still felt the sting of rejection acutely. One romance that ended before it started was with Rita Moreno. He made a date with her and promised her it would be a big, romance-filled night out. When Elvis showed up accompanied by four other guys, Rita took one look, told him he could go fly a kite—with his buddies—and went back inside the house.

Elvis occasionally got more entangled than he planned on. One costar who pursued him with single-minded vigor was Nancy Sinatra, the female lead of *Speedway*. For once, Elvis made an attempt to stay clear of an involvement, mostly out of the fear he still had of her father. But as long as it wasn't one of his ladies, Frank couldn't have cared less who Elvis slept with.

For Elvis, the affair with Nancy was a way to pass time, gratifying mostly because of how desperately he claimed she wanted him. But when the movie was over, he didn't give her another thought—until she showed up at Graceland a few weeks later, after he was no longer available for her calls. Elvis took her into the music room, and he was forced to break it off face to face, all along terrified Priscilla would find out who was there and grill him on it. Nancy eventually left, and for months, Elvis said he had nightmares of Frank coming to get him.

Juggling his affairs was more stressful with Priscilla than it had ever been with Gladys. He was always looking for ways to keep her at Graceland and keep his secret life secret. After Priscilla graduated from high school, Elvis insisted she enroll in finishing school, so she would be ready to face the public. But between the newspaper reports of his flings and the extended periods of separation, Priscilla grew impatient with his frequent departures and began to complain that she never got to see him. While her worries about his fidelity made him tired, her added complaints about his entourage eventually sparked a more violent reaction.

Elvis believed he was giving Priscilla everything she could possibly want—nice clothes, a beautiful place to live, servants to wait on her, expensive jewelry, and a future with him. He simply expected unconditional love in return. While the intensity of his feelings for Priscilla was just as strong, her increased complaints smacked of sheer betrayal, wounding and infuriating him.

Equally as upsetting for Elvis was the return of his broodiness and the ache of hollowness in the pit of his stomach. He silently blamed it on Priscilla—if she'd just love him and not try to *control* him, he wouldn't feel this way. She was letting him down, and it made him angry and mean.

Although nobody thought much about it, Elvis was never without several prescriptions for sleeping pills and tranquilizers. After all, if the doctors said it was okay, then it must be okay. But his reliance on the pills and the amount he took kept gradually increasing as his body gave in to the addiction, a silent weed overgrowing his soul. There were plenty of signs that a terrible transformation was taking place, but they were excused, overlooked, and ignored by everyone.

One side effect was sudden flashes of temper, as if his brain would suddenly short circuit and fire off a tension-relieving torpedo. In 1963 while he was filming *Fun in Acapulco*—shot, of course, in Hollywood he rented a house on Bellagio Road in Bel Air and made it a depot of activity. Priscilla was back in Memphis being baby-sat by Vernon and Dee.

One late afternoon Elvis was shooting pool with several of his buddies, who now traveled everywhere with him. One of the guys had brought a girl he had met at a bar earlier that day back to the house. She had followed in her car and was excited to be under the same roof as Elvis. But he was in one of his moods—edgy and inhospitable. When the girl was introduced, Elvis grunted a hello then asked her to leave.

She was very nervous and uncomfortable and wanted to leave, but a car was blocking hers in the driveway. When she came back to the game room to ask if the car could be moved, Elvis became furious. He picked up the white cue ball and threw it at her with all his might. It hit her with a sickening thud directly above her left breast. The force of the blow knocked her down, and it was obvious she was badly hurt. Elvis simply walked out of the room, looking disgusted.

The others tended to the girl for quite a while, until she was calmed down and capable of moving. Someone drove her home in her car, with another of Elvis's gang following behind in another car.

It had become Elvis's policy never to apologize. He hadn't uttered an "I'm sorry" to anyone for anything since Gladys's funeral. His way of saying he was sorry was to buy a present or give money to the person. While not everyone can be so easily bought, the girl didn't sue or go to the press with the story. Maybe if she had, it would have forced Elvis to take stock of himself right then and to own up to how much he'd changed in the last five years. It had happened bit by bit, day after day, so nobody noticed very much, especially not him.

Dominating his thoughts that year was the fear of becoming a footnote in music history. The British Invasion and four shaggy-haired youths from Liverpool were changing the face of music in America. Since Elvis's return from the army, his appeal had steadily moved into the mainstream, pushed along with the help of his unthreatening movie image and his association with polyester-clad Vegas. With the sixties loosening the moral constraints, he wasn't the controversial symbol of repressed youth anymore. Although Elvis wasn't yet 30, his career had entered middle age, throwing him into an early midlife crisis.

His records still sold well enough, his movies made money, and the casinos packed them in for performances, but he had lost his identity. On the road during his early days with RCA, Elvis was the leader of the pack, the Outlaw of Love in black. By the mid-1960s, he was known mostly as a star of bad movies he bitterly referred to as travelogues. "Stupid scripts that have me singing stupid songs," he said in disgust.

He occasionally had input on the songs he recorded, but the final decision still lay in others' hands, and Elvis blamed Parker for much of his predicament. "I begged that old man to let me do something different, but he won't because he doesn't think I can do any better."

Elvis's impatience with Parker had boiled over several times, and on two different occasions, after staying up all night and working himself into a rage, he actually fired the Colonel. The first time, Vernon nearly got hysterical. But he needn't have gotten so worked up, because Parker simply laughed off the threat. Each time Elvis tried to make the break and take more control in his life, he eventually backed down out of fear and insecurity, under pressure from the mysterious hold Parker exerted over him. Elvis would shake his head and bury his face in his hands. "Parker's got me by the balls. Ain't nothing I can do."

So his surges of independence never lasted; they merely precipitated orgies of hedonistic indulgence, the one thing he felt complete control over. Elvis played a dangerous emotional game of disassociating his emotions from his body's actions, and he was careless with the feelings of others. In one instance, it came back to haunt him mercilessly.

Among the many fellow actors and performers who would often seek to meet him backstage or at Graceland was Nick Adams. Nick was the star of *The Rebel* TV series, and Elvis was impressed Nick had sought him out. He and Elvis hit it off, and Nick was a regular friend. He called and wrote regularly and flew to Graceland a couple of times. He and Elvis would go motorcycle riding late at night and stay up until all hours talking about the pain of celebrity. They also shared a mutual enjoyment of prescription drugs.

Whenever Elvis flew into Hollywood, he made sure Nick knew, and Nick became a regular at whatever house Elvis was renting. Elvis still hated sleeping alone, and he grew close enough to Nick to ask him to stay over on nights he was feeling particularly blue but not up to a sexual confrontation with a woman. Although Elvis still enjoyed sleeping with two or more women, he seldom did anymore because he found it difficult to have more than one encounter a night—or sometimes even one. In addition to Elvis just getting older, the pills he took most certainly affected his sexual performance.

A few years later, in 1968, when it had been a long while since anyone remembered hearing from Nick, a phone call came with the news that he had died in his Coldwater Canyon home from an apparent drug overdose. Elvis's immediate reaction was to sit on the steps, frozen and mute.

His eyes welled with tears and his body shook as he rocked himself back and forth, arms clutching his sides.

Elvis was devastated and suffered through it for days. He sequestered himself upstairs and could be heard crying through the closed door. To calm himself, he took some tranquilizers and then sought out Earl to confess.

"He felt responsible for helping send Nick off the deep end and was punishing himself for it," Greenwood recalled. "Elvis talked about how close they had been, particularly after a couple of foursomes, and admitted he had 'spurned' Nick's friendship later, saying he had needed 'room to breathe,' because Nick had wanted 'too much, ya know?'"

It has since been speculated in Hollywood gossip that Presley and Adams may have shared some sort of intimate encounter. But there's no definitive evidence one way or another. And regardless of any intimacies, Nick Adams didn't kill himself over Elvis—even though Elvis beat himself up over Nick's death for a long time.

As always, performing was his saving grace. He never held back on stage and always gave his all when performing, working hard to please the fans so they would love him back. Singing to strangers in a darkened showroom or arena was the purest form of making love for Elvis, because it was the one time he was willing to completely surrender himself to another and expose his needs and vulnerability. People walking out after an Elvis concert swam in an afterglow of emotional intimacy.

While he grappled with figuring out his professional niche, Elvis felt he was being put under the gun concerning marriage. He accused Priscilla of trying to back him into a corner and Vernon for aiding and abetting her. Vernon was worried Priscilla would come to her senses and go find someone who would treat her properly. But Elvis didn't understand what the rush was; as far as he was concerned, they had the rest of their lives together.

Plus, in the early days of his career, Elvis cultivated the notion that his career would suffer if he was "unavailable." He believed a major part of his appeal was the fantasy that he was anyone's for the taking. With his career already in danger of being permanently mired in "travelogue" movies and middle-of-the-road songs, he didn't want to rock the boat further. Nor did he want to give up the image he had of himself as the Outlaw of Love, the restless spirit. Settling down as a husband would effectively and permanently close that chapter of his life at a time when he felt the most alive and vital.

He was also afraid of the commitment of being a husband and worried that the constraints would get in the way of the time and attention he paid to his career. A sidebar to that was the matter of infidelity—if you weren't married, technically it wasn't cheating.

When he was home, Elvis avoided the issue by spending as much time with his entourage as he did with Priscilla. For the most part, he still treated her like a china doll in front of others, even if she made him madder than hell with what he considered unreasonable complaints. The constant presence of his gang became a bone of contention. Priscilla wasn't the only one who resented them—Vernon considered them all users and hangers-on. Their function was to be at Elvis's beck and call, acting as errand boys, party partners, occasional pimps, late-night companions, and whipping boards. Except for Red, who'd been there from the beginning.

While Vernon's main gripe was financial, Priscilla let Elvis know she resented the time he devoted to them instead of her. He construed her loneliness as criticism, which infuriated him. The irony is that as much as Elvis yearned for a buddy network and paid through the nose to have one, he never trusted the guys who comprised his gang. He suspected each and every one would make a mad dash for the door if he went bankrupt, and because of that expectation, he often treated them cruelly, finding reasons to insult or embarrass them. If Elvis got it in his head that one of the guys had made a cutting remark or committed some other sin, like greed, he would fire him at the snap of a finger; each knew there was a waiting list of guys to take his place. Even Red wasn't immune from Elvis's distrust, although he had always been a most faithful friend and employee. The drugs whipped Elvis's imagination up into a frenzy.

Elvis attempted to mollify Priscilla and make peace by allowing her to come visit him in Hollywood while he was making another forgettable movie. Priscilla was delighted to be out of Graceland and in California with Elvis, but her happiness turned bitter as Elvis left her alone and still saw other women, even though Priscilla was waiting for him at home. The trip turned into a disaster, and the bad feelings on both sides erupted into a terrible fight.

The argument started with Priscilla accusing Elvis of running around behind her back, humiliating her. Guilty as sin, Elvis responded with fury that she dare question him about anything he did.

"I am so tired of *everybody* trying to control my every move. I don't know why she torments me like this," Elvis said later. "I thought she loved me enough to be different, but I keep forgetting, she's just like other women. I wanted to strangle her to shut her up, and that's the truth."

Instead, he attacked her clothes, shredding them. After he vented his fury on her wardrobe, Elvis grabbed Priscilla and threw her out into the driveway, tossing the destroyed garments after her. Sobbing, Priscilla collapsed in the driveway, confused as to what she had ever done to make him treat her this way. Elvis paced the front room, but as the sounds of Priscilla's cries filtered in, he ran outside and knelt down beside her, holding her and begging her forgiveness. He lifted her in his arms and took her inside, and then he came back and picked up the clothes. It was as if he were two different people, each fighting to overpower the other.

In 1964, Elvis starred in *Viva Las Vegas* with Ann-Margret. There was an immediate attraction between them, and as Elvis craved someone to get his mind off his dissatisfaction with his career and his anger at feeling railroaded into marrying Priscilla, it was inevitable they would have an affair. Their relationship was passionate, intense—and volatile.

In the beginning, Elvis was totally smitten and didn't care who knew it. Part of the initial appeal, as with the other actresses he'd dated, was Ann-Margret's standing within the Hollywood community. Despite the number of films he'd made and his status as a superstar with movie fans around the world, Elvis never felt truly accepted in the movie community. Maybe through Ann-Margret he could finally gain acceptance. Her genuine sweetness, along with her sexiness, drew Elvis to her. She was with Elvis because she truly cared about him, and he sensed she didn't care how much money he made or who he was.

Ann-Margret was the kind of woman who brought out the best and the worst in Elvis. Wanting to impress her and needing to feel worthy of her attention, he turned on the charm and let his boyish, vulnerable side show. He won her over with his sense of humor, one of his better qualities. She was an independent, self-assured woman—the type of female that frightened Elvis to death and made him feel inferior and threatened. That inner conflict made for much pain and many emotional scenes, probably more on her part than on his.

This was one of his more public affairs insofar as the amount of time they spent together and his "faithfulness" to her—during that time, she was the only woman he saw. It didn't take long for Priscilla to find out, and there wasn't much she could do but ride it out while Elvis wrestled with his predicament. Someone older or someone who didn't love Elvis as much would have probably told him to take a permanent hike, but not Priscilla. Then again, he kept her isolated and dependent, so she wasn't in the best position to walk. And in his egocentricity, he naïvely never considered the possibility he was forcing her into the arms of other men.

Elvis vacillated between the two women for a long time. Ann-Margret affected Elvis, and he wasn't able to shake her the way he had other affairs. If he hadn't been so tied up with insecurities, he might have fallen for her all the way. Other than Priscilla and Dixie, Ann-Margret was one of the loves of Elvis's life. But when they met, he was carrying too much baggage and he was too scared to change horses midstream. Priscilla was safe and more manageable, or so he thought, and much less scary.

The excuse to end his affair with Ann-Margret presented itself when a picture of the two of them appeared in a local Los Angeles paper, identifying them officially as an "item." Elvis convinced himself she had arranged for the photographer in order to force him into choosing between her and Priscilla. He had been in Hollywood long enough to know that half the publicity generated was at the urging of the studio or on the part of an enterprising photographer, but this scenario suited his needs.

He got himself so worked up with images of her betrayal that he needed to calm down with some Quaaludes, which had been prescribed by one of his doctors. Once their soothing effect took hold, he called Priscilla and acted as if nothing out of the ordinary had happened. Despite his tirade, Elvis found it difficult to tear himself away from Ann and continued to see her over the next few months. But for all intents and purposes, the relationship died that afternoon, and it wouldn't be long before he'd finally make Priscilla his wife.

Elvis and Priscilla were married in the Las Vegas fishbowl instead of the privacy of Graceland. After the briefest of honeymoons, the only thing marriage changed was Priscilla's name, because Elvis wouldn't and couldn't give up his affairs. He felt suffocated by his personal and professional life, the only release being the high of a new conquest and the comfort of tension-killing drugs. Exactly nine months after the wedding date, Lisa Marie was born; but not even his daughter could stop her father's self-destruction.

Chapter 14

A TRAGIC END

Frustrated at his stagnating career, Elvis gathered his resources and told Parker he wanted to go on tour again, yearning to get that old feeling of the road back. Parker ran with the idea and announced it to the press as a comeback tour—a notion irritating Elvis to no end. "He's making it sound like I'm a has-been."

Parker convinced Elvis it was a publicity ploy, something to make people take special notice. The King was going to reestablish his place as not just a singer, rock star, and movie idol, but as one of the great all-around entertainers *ever*. This appealed to Elvis so much that he wanted to take it even further: he wanted to go on a world tour.

Parker wouldn't hear of it. Elvis argued himself blue in the face to no avail—he didn't know about Parker's illegal immigrant status and assumed it was just another case of the Colonel's controlling him. Elvis ranted, raved, pouted, and claimed this latest run-in with Parker left such a sour taste in his mouth about the tour that he was of the mind to cancel the whole thing. But once the rehearsals were arranged, Elvis felt the itch to perform and devoted his full energies to preparing a terrific show.

The one who suffered was Priscilla. Elvis was preoccupied and didn't see how she was languishing for his time and attention. Not even the news she was pregnant made him reach up and take her off the pedestal and bring her beside him. He simply didn't treat her like a real woman. Plus, he left the impression that while their sex life was warm, it wasn't exciting enough for him, nor did he pursue it with much vigor. After waiting so many years for the proper time to consummate their relationship, he remained beset with the subconscious conflict of the Gladys/Priscilla idol he had constructed.

The comeback "tour" ended up being a much-ballyhooed concert in Hawaii. Elvis received an enthusiastic reception, but not much else came from it that affected his movie or recording career or selection. The movie scripts sent to him were still mindless pap, his records weren't climbing to the top of the charts, and knowing Las Vegas was still a stronghold only served to depress him more. He dealt with his frustration by lashing out at those around him.

Understanding what fueled his torment didn't make it any more palatable to those he abused, and for Earl Greenwood, it became increasingly harder to justify tacitly condoning it by his continued involvement as Elvis's publicist.

"There were always so many traumas and dramas covering for Elvis with yet another girl," Earl recalled. "Not that the affair itself gave him any happiness, but the danger and intrigue did; screening telephone calls; avoiding Priscilla lest she ask an embarrassing question; feeling the resentment of his entourage because of the bond Elvis and I had; seeing the pill bottles multiply on his nightstand; and watching Elvis compromise himself almost every step of the way, thinking one thing and acting as if he thought another."

Elvis never learned that it was okay to get mad at people directly, and that having it out and working through it let off constructive steam. Elvis feared that anger might lead to his rejection. The only people he felt in control enough to confront and overpower were his hired boys. Since he paid their way, he felt he owned them.

But just as difficult as Elvis's emotional insecurities was his lifestyle. "When he was home, he stayed up till all hours, able to sleep late into the afternoon the next day," says Greenwood. "But for those of us who had work to do, it took tremendous stamina to overcome the lack of sleep. Everything put together was taking a tremendous toll on me. My health suffered as did my enjoyment of doing Elvis's publicity, and finally one day, I woke up and admitted to myself what I'd been trying to avoid: I needed a break from the whirlwind that was Elvis Presley, Star. It was time to move on."

Elvis was also embarking on a new road—parenthood. After Lisa Marie was born on February 1, 1968, Elvis doted on and spoiled his little daughter beyond imagining. She was perfect and she was his spitting image. For a while, just looking at her overwhelmed him with emotion and chased away his torment. But as the newness wore off, the powerful hold of his drug dependency tightened its grip.

Elvis was living a self-fulfilling prophecy that he would be left alone because he did his best to drive people away. He had always placed all his eggs in any one given basket: if he were rich enough, he'd be happy; if only he had Priscilla to take care of him, he'd be happy; marriage would make everything perfect between him and Priscilla, and he'd be happy; being a father would change the world, and he'd be happy. However, money hadn't changed his background; Priscilla fell short of the unreasonable image he had created; she betrayed his trust by complaining and standing up for herself, proving she didn't love him unconditionally; Lisa Marie was precious, but Elvis was too needy to experience the true riches of having a child; his career had been a disappointment, and he felt used and taken by everyone around him.

He had grown up believing happiness and fulfillment could come from others, instead of realizing it must first come from within. Everything he had expected to fill the emptiness inside him had failed him. He was angry at the world but held himself in greater disdain—if he'd been worthy enough, his expectations would have been met. He turned ever more self-indulgent as his self-pity consumed him.

The most shocking side effect was his sudden lack of vanity about his appearance, and the extra weight he gained didn't seem to bother him. It was a combination of drug abuse and self-punishment, and indicated a certain amount of surrender—he was on the verge of giving up altogether. Still, Elvis maintained he could lose the weight anytime he wanted by increasing the number of karate lessons he took each week, and he claimed he was just relaxing and enjoying the fruits of his years of hard labor.

His weight and bloat kept him from being wooed by Hollywood, but his appearance didn't put a damper on his affairs. And Lisa Marie provided Elvis with the perfect excuse to leave Priscilla behind. The double standard within him was so fixed, it didn't occur to him that Priscilla might get lonely enough to have affairs of her own, which in fact she did because Elvis refused to have sex with her now that she was a mother. In the same way that Gladys and poverty had robbed Elvis of his childhood, Elvis stole Priscilla's adolescence by shutting her up in Graceland. The time had come for Priscilla to try out her wings.

One of her passions became karate. Through Elvis, she hooked up with an instructor he knew named Mike Stone, to give her private lessons. On the few occasions that Elvis let Priscilla and Lisa Marie travel with him, it wasn't unusual for Stone to show up and give them instruction, which Elvis thought nothing of. He trusted Priscilla for a number of reasons: he kept her pretty well isolated, his sexual ego wouldn't dream of her infidelity, and in his mind she was simple and pure and not driven by thoughts of the flesh.

While Priscilla strove to create her own emotional life, Elvis plodded through his. He grew increasingly paranoid about the press and developed a phobia that people were literally out to get him. For protection, he began carrying a gun, loving the sense of power it gave him.

His paranoia wasn't relegated to the press and faceless would-be assassins. Anyone around him was suspect, as was shockingly proven when he summarily fired Red.

Jealousies abounded among the men in Elvis's entourage, with power plays and cliques the norm. Red was loyal through and through and not devious enough to watch his own back. Somewhere along the line, somebody put a bug in Elvis's ear that led him to decide Red was just using him. Betrayal and treachery would not be tolerated, and Elvis abruptly cut him off. He refused to give a reason and got into a heated argument with Vernon that ended with Elvis reminding him who held the purse strings. Even Red was at a loss as to why Elvis cut him off so abruptly. But once Elvis let go, there was no coming back, and West went the way of so many others.

It is more than a little ironic that Elvis despised hippies because they smoked marijuana and dropped acid. It elevated to a theater of the absurd when Elvis arranged to visit President Nixon in October 1970 to offer his help in the war on drugs. Stoned out of his mind on pills, Elvis was escorted to the Oval Office, where he railed against drugs. Nixon listened politely and then gave Elvis a federal Drug Enforcement Administration (DEA) officer's badge as part of a photo op. Back home, the DEA badge was kept in a drawer beside the one that held his medications.

In 1971, Elvis was appearing at the Sahara Club in Tahoe and saw a girl who knocked him off his feet. She wore minimal makeup but was very pretty. Elvis made lots of flirtatious eye contact and sang half of his songs directly to her. Immediately after the show she was escorted—minus her mother—back to Elvis's hotel suite. She stayed with him throughout the rest of his Tahoe engagement, and he liked her so much that he risked taking her with him to his home in Palm Springs.

Elvis's usage of prescription drugs had branched out to include more than just sleeping pills. Painkillers and depressants of various types were taken carelessly, and even a narcotic, Hycodan, entered the picture. Elvis took some pills and gave the girl some as well before retiring to his room.

The next day, Elvis was later than usual getting up. One of his group knocked on the bedroom door for several minutes and, when there was no answer, walked in. Elvis was groggy, trying to respond to the knocking. The girl was lying very still, unconscious. They tried waking her up, and when she didn't respond, they panicked.

Some of the guys insisted an ambulance be called immediately, but the others were afraid. Eventually, good sense won out. They called the paramedics and then dragged Elvis out of bed and threw him into a cold shower to clear out the cobwebs. By the time the medics got there, Elvis was dressed and alert. Aware of what was going on and informed of the girl's precarious state, Elvis wasn't overly concerned. He stayed in the back room reading until the ambulance left, then sent out for pizza.

She remained in intensive care for several days, lingering between life and death. Elvis never once went to see her, and he never once called. She pulled through, and when she was released, a return ticket to Lake Tahoe was waiting for her. He made it a point not to be available for any communication with her after that.

Elvis got careless and less discreet with his affairs, tormenting Priscilla by flaunting his other women. Obviously, he wanted her to know, to punish her for failing him and to test the strength of her professed love. Once he *accidentally* forgot to destroy a note sent by one of his flings, who signed it Lizard Tongue.

He ducked Priscilla's accusation of infidelity by swearing the letter was from a crazy fan who sent it after a concert. He deluded himself into believing Priscilla bought that story and was over her anger and humiliation. He ran out of alibis the night Priscilla caught him red-handed in Palm Springs. She drove down to the desert resort with a girlfriend from Los Angeles and barged into the house. Some of Elvis's guys tried to stop her or call out a warning, but she was on fire and not to be messed with.

When she burst into the bedroom, Elvis responded with his own fury, incensed that Priscilla *dare* check up on him—the illogic of his argument exasperating. They screamed at each other, hurling slurs and accusations. The incident didn't immediately break them up, but it did slash an irreparable tear in the fabric of their relationship.

In California, Elvis owned a house in the exclusive Holmby Hills, and it was from one of the maids there that word first got out that Priscilla and Mike Stone were having an affair. By that time, she and Stone had been involved for nearly two years. The news made Vernon nervous. He couldn't blame Priscilla—he'd been after Elvis for years with dire warnings that he was going to lose his pretty, vivacious wife if he didn't take better care of her. But Elvis was still his son, and he sensed how close to the edge he was. He prayed Priscilla would somehow stick with the marriage. If she didn't, he was afraid it would literally kill Elvis.

Vernon's prayers were not answered. In early 1972, Priscilla showed up unannounced in Las Vegas. Right before Elvis was to perform, she told him that she was leaving with Lisa Marie. Then she left him to wallow in his disbelief and humiliation. Elvis was in a state of shock but never considered cancelling the show, and that night he gave one of his most affecting performances ever. He bled for his fans; had he shown Priscilla half as much emotion, they'd have still been together.

After the performance, Elvis had a meltdown of mythic proportions. He alternated among rage and confusion and despair. He simply couldn't understand what Priscilla felt he hadn't given her, and he threatened to have her lover killed. That she had left him for Mike Stone, a man he considered a friend, merely exacerbated his paranoia.

He obsessed on Stone. He once shot up the TV when *The Streets of San Francisco* came on, because one of the characters was named Mike Stone. And his threat to kill Stone was more than a passing fantasy. In a moment of drug-addled madness, Elvis *had* ordered someone to arrange a hit on Stone; but after some time to reflect and sober up, he dropped the idea.

Throughout the period between their separation and the divorce, Elvis never gave up hope that Priscilla would come back to him. He called her constantly and tried to win her over with shared memories and a belief they were each other's destiny, but she wouldn't be swayed. Elvis took his anger and frustration at Priscilla's rejection out on whoever happened to be in his path.

He developed an intense dislike and resentment of other entertainers. Robert Goulet was a favorite target, as was Pat Boone. One time when Elvis was in Vegas, Goulet came on the TV during dinner. Elvis picked up a gun and shot the TV, causing it to explode, glass flying everywhere— then calmly put the gun back down and continued eating.

He pulled a gun on Jimmy Dean, after the easygoing country singer joked about how long he had to wait for Elvis's security to clear him backstage. Nothing he did changed the fact that he had lost Priscilla, and they were divorced in California during the fall of 1973.

On the day they went to court, his moods were swinging wildly between depression and fury. At one point, he reached out and held her hand, begging her not to go through with it. He couldn't believe she was really leaving. Outside the courtroom, reality began to sink in, and Elvis shook with fury. He reached into his pocket, grabbed a handful of cash, and threw it at her. "That's all she ever wanted from me, anyway. I gave her everything but it wasn't enough. Nothing ever been enough."

Six months after Priscilla moved out to live with Mike Stone, Elvis met a beautiful university student named Linda Thompson. They would end up dating for more than four years, with Thompson living at Graceland for part of that time. She would later paint a dreary picture of life with Elvis as his health suffered. "Elvis was in the hospital a couple of times with pneumonia and other health problems. I stayed in the hospital with him for two and a half weeks at a time. I had my own hospital bed that was pushed up against his." Thompson added she "found it sad to watch him self-destruct."[1]

But Elvis deluded himself that he wasn't a drug abuser, because his pills and liquids were prescription medicines, doled out by doctors in response to Elvis's complaints of stress and insomnia. On a trip, his suitcases were loaded with dozens of little orange bottles filled with a myriad of pills, and at home his medicine cabinets were a cornucopia of pharmaceuticals.

When Elvis was under the influence of whatever drug was his favorite at the moment, one could expect the unexpected. One afternoon Elvis and a couple of his buddies went to have some prescriptions refilled at his favorite pharmacy. Elvis was upbeat, almost manic, that day and in the mood for company. The pharmacist, who was a big fan, loved showing off to his customers that Elvis Presley was a friend—so much so that on a couple of occasions the pharmacist let Elvis don his coat and hand out prescriptions to startled customers. Elvis would laugh like a little kid at the double takes he got and would stand behind the counter for hours.

It seemed like harmless fun, but the joke masked a mind and soul that were racing out of control. In public situations like that, Elvis was usually expert at hiding the turmoil beneath the surface. But periodically his mood would abruptly turn black, stunning those who were unaware of his chemically induced emotional swings and causing Elvis to hurry home and shut himself in his room, often for days or weeks on end.

The drugs Elvis took to calm himself actually exacerbated his feelings of vulnerability and insecurity. His greatest fear was being poor, and Elvis dwelt upon it constantly. On more than one occasion, he took handfuls of jewels and cash into the backyard of Graceland and buried them, little treasures to call on should he suddenly find himself penniless. Certain members of his entourage would watch Elvis digging in the dark, trying to ward off his worst nightmare.

They didn't try to stop him, because on one hand, they knew how violent Elvis could become if someone got in his way; and on the other, they knew full well that Elvis would remember nothing of his handiwork by the time he woke up the following afternoon. Once they were convinced he had forgotten his buried treasure, they would dig it up and split the stash among themselves. It's no wonder he used to say he never felt he could truly trust anyone.

Elvis's last chance at salvation came during 1975 in the unlikely form of Barbra Streisand. She and Jon Peters flew to Las Vegas and asked Elvis to costar in the remake of *A Star Is Born*. Elvis couldn't believe it—the chance to work with a real actress in a real movie and not some "travelogue," where the only thing that changes is the scenery. Playing a broken-down rock star appealed to him; it wasn't just a role, it was his life. He could pour everything into it.

As far as he was concerned, it was a done deal and he was already making plans. He arranged to take acting lessons and told the cook to take it easy on the fried foods, although his bloated appearance suited the character. He turned the negotiations over to Parker with more than a little smugness. Elvis was so sure he had the role sewn up, he checked himself into a Memphis hospital under an assumed name, under the cover of darkness, to get a facelift. The vanity of it all wasn't lost on him, but he didn't care, because visions of a career rebirth danced merrily in his head.

There is some disagreement as to what happened next. According to Greenwood, the Colonel was insulted that Streisand approached Elvis directly. So he intentionally blew the deal by asking for only Elvis's name above the title and a million dollars. Parker then told Elvis that Streisand changed her mind and decided to go with the more popular Kris Kristofferson. "He didn't discover the truth until after the movie had been made, when a studio lawyer came to visit him backstage in Vegas. When he confronted Parker, the Colonel shrugged and said he'd find something better."

On the other hand, Sonny West claimed that Elvis backed out when getting in shape proved too difficult and then had the Colonel ask for too much money. The only problem with that scenario is that the contract would probably have been signed long before Elvis began working out.

In any event, Elvis never made another movie. His lost chance at returning to the top touched him to the very core of his soul. It festered inside him, and no amount of drugs or women could completely erase his sense of loss.

Regardless of the reason, Elvis gathered himself up and realized it was time to make the break. If he didn't do it now, he never would. He had spent his adult years going through a painful adolescence, and he was finally ready to assume responsibility for his life. Besides not wanting to fade away into a has-been, he wanted Lisa Marie to be proud of him. It was time to come clean and to stop running scared.

He put himself on the line and told several people he was going to fire Parker. And if Parker wanted to try to ruin him, so be it. He didn't have much left to lose as it was. He also confessed to the secret that had hung over his head like the sword of Damocles. In the liberal atmosphere of the 1970s it was hard to believe what Parker had used to control Elvis for the last 17 years—a week's worth of home movies of Elvis in bed with underage groupies.

Elvis told Greenwood that Parker either found the tapes or, more likely, had been paying one of his early hired hands or household staff to keep a special eye on Elvis. He had no idea who had betrayed him. But Parker had known as soon as Gladys died that he would need to find a new leverage. The day Elvis intended to lay down the law to Parker about the direction he wanted to take his career, Parker countered with a checkmate. With the Jerry Lee Lewis scandal fresh in everyone's mind—Lewis had married his 13-year-old cousin and nearly ruined his career—Parker convinced Elvis his career wouldn't be worth spit if those tapes made their way into the hands of the press. He had a hold on him and would tighten his grip anytime Elvis displayed a surge of independence.

Revealing the secret that had controlled his life proved cathartic, and Elvis felt a weight lift off his shoulders. He felt optimistic enough to begin a new exercise program and go on a diet. He was also smitten again, this time to a teenager named Ginger Alden. She had gotten his interest when she initially refused to move in with him. According to Vernon, Elvis proposed to Ginger by giving her an 11 1/2 carat diamond ring and had told his father that he wanted to have children with her.

He sought redemption, but the years of abuse had the final say and shut his body down before he had a chance to make the attempt. On August 16, 1977, Elvis was discovered on the floor of his Graceland bathroom and rushed to Baptist Memorial Hospital. He was pronounced dead on arrival. The cause of death was listed as a heart attack, but it was determined to be cardiac arrhythmia, an irregular heartbeat. In addition, the postmortem revealed an enlarged liver and a potpourri of drugs in his bloodstream, including extremely high levels of methoqualone, or Quaaludes, and codeine.

Elvis was right about one thing—his death wasn't the end. It was the beginning of what would become a multimillion-dollar enterprise that ensures his immortality. His image is carefully licensed, and Graceland is now a tourist attraction, but his legacy is still debated. That's because like Van Gogh, whose visions resulted in both beautiful paintings and the madness that caused him to cut off his own ear, the very qualities that made Elvis a performer for the ages had also worked to destroy him.

In the end it is that dichotomy that continues to fascinate—even the post office couldn't decide whether to have his postage stamp portray the leather-clad 1950s rebel or the pill-popping 1970s lounge singer. The fact is, he was both. What should be remembered most is how much he accomplished in spite of his debilitating insecurities and self-destructive behavior. Only by embracing the flawed man behind the public image can his contribution to music and American culture be truly appreciated and celebrated both now and for generations to come.

NOTE

1. Andrew Hearn, interview with Linda Thompson, Elvis Presley Australia, http://www.elvis.com.au/presley/interview_lindathompson.shtml.

FURTHER READING

Curtin, Jim, with Renata Ginter. *Elvis: Unknown Stories behind the Legend*. Nashville, TN: Celebrity Books, 1998.

Daily, Robert. *The King of Rock 'n' Roll*. New York: Franklin Watts, 1996.

Gordon, Robert. *The Elvis Treasures*. New York: Villard, 2002.

Guralnick, Peter. *Careless Love: The Unmaking of Elvis Presley*. Boston: Little Brown & Co., 1999.

Hopkins, Jerry. *Elvis—The Final Years*. New York: Berkley Publishing Group, 1985.

Jorgensen, Ernst. *A Life in Music—The Complete Recording Sessions*. New York: St. Martin's Griffin, 2000.

Lichter, Paul. *Elvis in Hollywood*. New York: Simon & Schuster, 1975.

Mann, Alan. *Elvis and Buddy*. York, England: Music Mentor Books, 2002.

Mason, Bobbie Ann. *Elvis Presley: A Penguin Life*. New York: Viking Penguin, 2003.

Nash, Alanna, with Bill Smith, Marty Lacker, and Lamar Fike. *Elvis Aaron Presley: Revelations from the Memphis Mafia*. New York: HarperCollins, 1995.

Osborne, Jerry. *Elvis Word for Word*. New York: Harmony Books, 1999.

Presley, Priscilla Beaulieu, and Sandra Harmon. *Elvis and Me*. New York: Putnam, 1985.

Presley, Priscilla, Lisa Marie Presley, and David Ritz (Editor). *Elvis by the Presleys*. New York: Crown, 2005.

Vellenga, Dirk, with Mick Farren. *Elvis and the Colonel*. New York: Bantam Books, 2002.

WEB SITES

Elvis Presley: The Official Web Site for Elvis Presley, *All About Elvis*, http://www.elvis.com/elvisology/

Rock and Roll Hall of Fame Museum, *Elvis Presley*, http://www.rockhall.com/hof/inductee.asp?id = 171

Elvis Australia, Official Elvis Presley Fan Club, http://www.elvis.com.au/

INDEX

About the Author

KATHLEEN TRACY is a Los Angeles–based journalist. She is the author of more than 20 titles, including *The Boy Who Would Be King: An Intimate Portrait of Elvis Presley by His Cousin* (1990). Her work has also been featured in *A&E Biography* magazine and *Variety*.